I0020271

Legal Disclaimer and Copyright Notice

This book is provided for informational purposes only and does not constitute legal advice or professional consultation. The strategies, recommendations, and insights within this book are based on the author's experience and the information available at the time of writing, including validations against artificial intelligence platforms such as ChatGPT for accuracy. The field of **Cybersecurity** is rapidly evolving, and while every effort has been made to ensure the information in this book is current and accurate, technologies, standards, and threats change over time. Therefore, this book should serve as a general guide rather than an exhaustive source of the latest **Cybersecurity** practices.

Readers are encouraged to consult with professional **Cybersecurity** specialists for advice tailored to their specific circumstances. The author and publisher disclaim any liability for any direct, indirect, incidental, or consequential damages resulting from the use of the information in this book.

About the Author

In the dynamic expanse of the technological landscape, my journey has been an exploration through fields of innovation, over obstacles of challenge, and across the diverse terrains of change. With each step, I've accumulated a rich tapestry of skills, not merely as accolades but as essential tools. These tools have enabled me to navigate the complexities of the digital domain, to construct, to safeguard, and to innovate. This document is a reflection of that journey, an odyssey that extends through the realms of **Cybersecurity**, network architecture, and software engineering.

Garnered through a variety of roles within technology, my expertise spans application security, vulnerability management, identity and access management (IAM), security information and event management (SIEM), infrastructure security, and the nuanced art of software engineering. These areas are not just professional jargon; they represent the foundational elements upon which I've built my understanding and approach to digital challenges, balancing the creation of secure, resilient systems with the development of impactful software solutions.

At my core, I am both a creator and guardian within the digital space. My efforts have established the groundwork for IT infrastructure, **Cybersecurity** measures, and software systems that are designed to be robust and adaptable to the challenges of digital disruption. This educational document aims to impart the insights I've garnered and the knowledge I've accumulated. It's crafted for the next generation of IT enthusiasts, **Cybersecurity** advocates, and software developers—those who share a passion for understanding and shaping the technological world.

Table of Contents

Introduction to **Cybersecurity**

Currently **Cybersecurity** encompasses a comprehensive, multi-layered defense strategy devised to protect data, networks, and devices from a wide array of digital attacks. In an era where information is a paramount asset, the significance of **Cybersecurity** cannot be overstated. It serves as the fortress that guards against unauthorized access, data breaches, and malware, ensuring the integrity, confidentiality, and availability of data.

At its core, **Cybersecurity** is about establishing a secure environment where businesses and individuals can operate without fear of cyber threats compromising their digital assets. This involves a systematic approach that integrates various security measures and practices across different levels of the digital landscape. From deploying firewalls and anti-virus software to securing endpoints and educating users, every layer adds a critical piece to the overall security puzzle.

The ultimate goal of **Cybersecurity** is not just to defend against attacks but to create a robust infrastructure that can anticipate, withstand, and recover from threats, thereby maintaining the trust of stakeholders and protecting the reputation and operations of organizations. As cyber threats continue to evolve in complexity and sophistication, the role of **Cybersecurity** becomes increasingly vital, demanding constant vigilance, adaptation, and enhancement of security measures.

By understanding **Cybersecurity** as a dynamic and layered defense strategy, organizations and individuals can better prepare themselves against the ever-changing threat landscape, safeguarding their most valuable information assets in the digital age.

Through this book I will talk about different technologies you should have an understanding of and break down some of the basic security measures that should be put in place. At the bottom of certain sections I will bring up known breaches that happened due to that security layer being misconfigured or not there with some details about the breaches.

First, I will be starting out with breaking down the fundamental layers of cybersecurity with a brief description of each layer and then a section breaking down each section a bit more. Once you complete that chapter I will jump into

Fundamental Layers of **Cybersecurity**

Physical Security

The foundation of **Cybersecurity** starts with physical security, which protects the hardware and physical infrastructure that stores and transmits digital data. This includes securing data centers, offices, and computing hardware against unauthorized physical access, theft, and damage. Physical security measures can include locks, biometric scanners, security guards, and surveillance systems.

Network Security

This layer aims to protect the integrity, usability, and safety of network and data. Network security includes hardware and software technologies designed to prevent unauthorized access, misuse, malfunction, modification, destruction, or improper disclosure, creating a secure platform for computers, users, and programs to perform their permitted critical functions within a secure environment. Key components include firewalls, anti-virus software, intrusion detection and prevention systems (IDPS), and virtual private networks (VPNs) to encrypt data in transit.

Endpoint Security

Endpoint security refers to protecting the devices that connect to the network, such as computers, smartphones, and tablets. Endpoint security solutions help detect and block threats at the device level and can include anti-virus programs, anti-malware, and personal firewalls. Managing and securing these endpoints is crucial, as they are often the targets of initial attack attempts.

Application Security

Application security focuses on keeping software and devices free of threats. A compromised application could provide access to the data it's designed to protect. Security begins in the design phase, well before a program or device is deployed. Application security measures can include input validation to prevent SQL injection and cross-site scripting, authentication and authorization protocols, encryption, and security testing and updates.

Data Security

Data security protects data from unauthorized access, corruption, or theft throughout its lifecycle. It includes a range of technologies and processes such as encryption, tokenization, and data masking, along with access control mechanisms that ensure only authorized users can access specific data. Data loss prevention (DLP) strategies are also crucial to detect and prevent potential data breaches or data exfiltration transmissions.

Identity and Access Management (IAM)

IAM systems ensure that only authorized individuals can access certain technology resources, and only within the right context. This involves technologies for authentication (verifying who you are) and authorization (determining what resources you can access). IAM measures include multi-factor authentication, single sign-on systems, and user access reviews.

Incident Response

Despite best efforts to prevent them, breaches can and do occur. An incident response layer is critical for quickly addressing and mitigating the effects of an attack. This involves having a plan in place to detect, respond to, and recover from security incidents. The plan includes roles and responsibilities, communication protocols, and procedures for containing and eliminating threats.

User Education and Awareness

The human element is often considered the weakest link in **Cybersecurity**. Educating users about safe practices — such as recognizing phishing attempts, using strong passwords, and protecting sensitive information — is critical. Ongoing awareness training can significantly reduce the risk of successful attacks.

Overall, no single layer of **Cybersecurity** can protect against all potential threats. A layered, or defense-in-depth, approach ensures that when one defense perimeter is breached, additional layers of security protect the organization's data and systems. This comprehensive strategy is essential for effectively defending against the increasingly sophisticated range of **Cybersecurity** threats faced by organizations today.

Physical Security

Physical security is the protection of personnel, hardware, software, networks, and data from physical actions and events that could cause serious loss or damage to an enterprise, agency, or institution. This includes protection from fire, flood, natural disasters, burglary, theft, vandalism, and terrorism. It's the first line of defense in a comprehensive **Cybersecurity** strategy. Physical security is a foundational aspect of an organization's overall security posture. It not only protects against the physical theft of information but also supports **Cybersecurity** efforts by limiting the risk of unauthorized access to critical infrastructure and data. In today's increasingly interconnected world, neglecting physical security can lead to significant vulnerabilities and undermine the effectiveness of digital security measures.

Physical Security in **Cybersecurity**
Physical security is crucial for several reasons:

1. *Prevents Unauthorized Access*: By controlling physical access to buildings, data centers, and other critical infrastructure, organizations can prevent unauthorized individuals from accessing and potentially compromising sensitive information. Methods like locks, biometric scanners, security badges, and guard patrols are employed to ensure that only authorized personnel can enter certain locations.

2. *Protects Against Physical Damage*: Disasters, whether natural or man-made, can destroy hardware and infrastructure, leading to loss of data and services. Physical security measures such as fire suppression systems, earthquake-proofing, and flood defenses protect against such damage.

3. *Secures Against Data Theft*: Physical theft of devices like laptops, hard drives, and mobile devices can lead to significant security breaches. Physical security helps prevent such thefts and the potential loss of sensitive or proprietary information.

4. *Supports Cybersecurity Measures*: Physical security complements **Cybersecurity** efforts by adding an additional layer of protection. For example, securing physical access to networked devices helps prevent tampering that could bypass **Cybersecurity** measures.

5. *Regulatory Compliance*: Many regulations and standards, including HIPAA for healthcare and PCI DSS for payment card information, require certain levels of physical security to be in place to protect sensitive data. Compliance is not only a legal requirement but also helps in maintaining trust and credibility with customers and partners.

6. *Business Continuity and Recovery*: Physical security measures play a vital role in business continuity planning and disaster recovery. By protecting physical assets from damage or disruption, organizations can ensure that they are able to recover and resume operations more quickly after an incident.

Elements of Physical Security
Effective physical security encompasses several elements:

- Access Control: Mechanisms and policies that restrict access to physical locations to authorized personnel only. This can include locks, key cards, biometric systems, and security personnel.

- Surveillance: The use of cameras and monitoring equipment to oversee premises and detect unauthorized activities or individuals.

- Environmental Controls: Systems designed to protect equipment from environmental hazards, such as fire suppression systems, HVAC systems to control temperature and humidity, and protection against natural disasters.

- Security Policies and Training: Policies that define security procedures, responsibilities, and protocols. Training ensures that employees are aware of security policies and how to respond in case of an emergency.

Penetration testers often employ strategies to evaluate the robustness of an organization's physical security controls. A common tactic is to attempt tailgating, which involves following an authorized person into a secured area without being detected. Through my personal experience in penetration testing, I've employed several techniques to breach physical security measures. For instance, I've successfully left a Raspberry Pi device connected to an unoccupied network port under a desk. This device was configured to establish a VPN connection back to my network, granting me unrestricted access to the target network. Another innovative tool that's been utilized in the field is a USB keylogger, discreetly attached to the back of a docking station. This particular keylogger was equipped with a Wi-Fi hotspot, enabling the attacker to remotely collect login information from outside the building. These examples highlight the critical importance of both recognizing and reinforcing physical security measures to protect against unauthorized network access.

Network Security

Network security is a critical component of an organization's overall **Cybersecurity** strategy, focusing on protecting the integrity, confidentiality, and availability of data and resources that traverse and reside within the network infrastructure. It encompasses a set of policies, practices, and technologies designed to safeguard the network and data from unauthorized access, misuse, modification, or denial of service attacks.

Importance of Network Security
Network security is essential for several reasons:

1. Protection of Sensitive Data: Networks often carry sensitive, confidential, or proprietary information. Effective network security measures help protect this data from unauthorized access or interception, ensuring that it remains confidential and secure.

2. Maintaining Privacy: For businesses and individuals alike, privacy is a fundamental concern. Network security helps in maintaining the privacy of communications and data, which is especially critical in industries like healthcare and finance that handle highly sensitive information.

3. Ensuring Business Continuity: Cyberattacks or network disruptions can lead to significant downtime, affecting an organization's operations and reputation. Network security practices help ensure that services remain available, minimizing the risk of downtime and ensuring business continuity.

4. Regulatory Compliance: Many industries are subject to regulatory requirements that mandate the protection of sensitive data. Network security measures are critical to achieving compliance with laws and regulations such as GDPR, HIPAA, and PCI-DSS, helping avoid legal penalties and fines.

5. Protecting Against Threats: The cyber threat landscape is constantly evolving, with new threats emerging regularly. Network security helps protect against a wide array of threats, including malware, ransomware, phishing attacks, and more.

6. Building Trust: Effective network security measures build trust among customers, partners, and stakeholders by demonstrating a commitment to protecting sensitive information and ensuring reliable services.

The Role of Network Scanning in Network Security
Network scanning is a critical activity within network security, serving as both a diagnostic and a preventive measure. By actively probing a network, administrators can identify vulnerabilities, misconfigurations, and unauthorized devices that could pose a risk to the network's security. Here are key reasons why network scanning is integral to network security:

- Vulnerability Identification: Network scanning tools can discover vulnerabilities in the network infrastructure, such as open ports, outdated software versions, and vulnerabilities in network protocols.

- Network Inventory and Mapping: Scanning helps in creating a detailed inventory of all devices and services on the network, making it easier to manage and secure the network effectively.

- Compliance and Policy Enforcement: Regular scanning ensures that the network remains in compliance with internal policies and external regulatory requirements by identifying deviations from established security policies.

- Threat Detection: Advanced network scanning can detect signs of compromised devices or suspicious network activity, enabling timely response to potential threats.

By seamlessly integrating network scanning into their security practices, organizations can significantly enhance their network security posture, making their networks more resilient against cyber threats and ensuring the protection of critical data and resources.

The 2013 Target Corporation data breach stands as a stark example of network security vulnerabilities being exploited on a massive scale. In this incident, cyber attackers managed to exfiltrate around 40 million credit and debit card records, alongside 70 million records containing Target customers' personal information. The breach mechanism involved the installation of malware on Target's point-of-sale (POS) systems, enabling the theft of credit card data during transaction processing.

This security breach was initiated via a third-party vendor—an HVAC company—that possessed network access privileges for purposes like electronic billing and project management. The cybercriminals initially acquired the HVAC company's network credentials, leveraging this access as a pivot point into Target's network, despite this not being a breach of Target's physical premises. This situation underscores the critical role of securing all network access points, including those provided to third-party vendors for operational reasons.

Utilizing the compromised credentials, the attackers navigated through Target's network to its POS systems. This breach underscores the necessity for stringent security measures around network access, emphasizing that the security of systems peripheral to an organization's core digital infrastructure cannot be overlooked.

*The Target data breach serves as a cautionary tale about the deep interplay between physical security measures and **Cybersecurity** practices. It highlights the imperative for a holistic security strategy that rigorously addresses vulnerabilities, including those that might arise from relationships with external vendors and contractors, to safeguard sensitive information and systems effectively.*

Endpoint Security

Endpoint security refers to the practices and technologies used to protect endpoints or entry points of end-user devices such as desktops, laptops, and mobile devices from being exploited by malicious actors and campaigns. Endpoints serve as points of access to an enterprise network, creating potential entry points for security threats. Endpoint security aims to secure every endpoint connecting to a network to block access attempts and other risky activities at these points of entry.

Importance of Endpoint Security

The importance of endpoint security has grown significantly with the increase in mobile and remote working, the diversity of endpoint devices, and the sophistication of cyber threats. Here's why endpoint security is critical:

1. Growing Number of Endpoints: The proliferation of devices, including BYOD (Bring Your Own Device) policies, has expanded the attack surface for organizations. Each device with access to the network increases the potential for security breaches.

2. Advanced Threats: Cyber threats have become more sophisticated, employing tactics that can bypass traditional security measures. Advanced persistent threats (APTs), ransomware, and zero-day attacks specifically target endpoints as entry points into the network.

3. Data Protection: Endpoints often store sensitive data or have access to critical network resources. Protecting these devices is crucial to safeguarding intellectual property and personal information against theft or exposure.

4. Regulatory Compliance: Many industries are governed by regulations that require the protection of sensitive data. Endpoint security measures are vital for compliance with standards like

GDPR, HIPAA, and PCI DSS, which dictate how data should be securely processed and stored.

5. Remote Work Vulnerabilities: With more employees working remotely, devices are often connected to unsecured networks, increasing vulnerability to attacks. Endpoint security solutions can provide critical protection for devices outside the traditional network perimeter.

Components of Endpoint Security

Endpoint security encompasses various tools and techniques designed to detect, prevent, and respond to threats. Common components include:

- Antivirus and Anti-malware Software: Continuously scans and monitors endpoints for malware and removes any threats that are detected.

- Firewalls: Control incoming and outgoing network traffic based on an organization's security policies to prevent unauthorized access to endpoints.

- Endpoint Detection and Response (EDR): Provides real-time monitoring and collection of endpoint data with capabilities to quickly respond to threats. EDR solutions can identify suspicious activities and automate responses to detected threats.

- Application Control: Blocks unauthorized applications from executing in the first place, which helps prevent malicious software from running on endpoints.

- Encryption: Protects data stored on endpoints by converting it into unreadable code that cannot be easily deciphered by unauthorized users.

- Patch Management: Ensures that operating systems and applications are up-to-date with the latest patches, closing vulnerabilities that could be exploited by attackers.

Best Practices for Endpoint Security

Implementing a robust endpoint security strategy involves several best practices:

- Regularly Update and Patch Systems: Keeping software and operating systems updated is crucial to protect against known vulnerabilities.

- Implement Strong Authentication Methods: Use multi-factor authentication (MFA) to add an extra layer of security for accessing network resources.

- Educate Users: Regularly train employees on security best practices, phishing awareness, and safe internet usage to reduce the risk of user-induced security breaches.

- Use a Comprehensive Security Solution: Choose endpoint security solutions that offer integrated protection features to address a wide range of threats.

- Monitor and respond: Continuously monitor endpoints for suspicious activities and have a response plan in place to address detected threats quickly.

Endpoint security is a fundamental aspect of an organization's overall security posture, addressing the vulnerabilities and threats at the device level. In today's dynamic threat landscape, it's essential for protecting critical data and infrastructure against increasingly sophisticated cyberattacks.

An example of a breach resulting from endpoint security vulnerabilities is the WannaCry ransomware attack in May 2017. This global cyberattack targeted computers running the Microsoft Windows operating system by encrypting data and demanding ransom payments in the Bitcoin cryptocurrency. The attack exploited vulnerabilities in older, unpatched versions of Windows, affecting more than 200,000 computers across 150 countries. Critical infrastructure, including hospitals, banks, and government agencies, was hit, leading to .widespread disruption

The WannaCry outbreak underscored the importance of maintaining endpoint security through regular software updates and patches. Many of the affected systems were vulnerable because they were either running outdated versions of Windows that were no longer supported or had not applied recent security updates provided by Microsoft. This attack highlighted the critical need for organizations to implement comprehensive endpoint management policies, ensuring all devices are regularly updated to protect against known vulnerabilities and .threats

In response to the attack, Microsoft released emergency patches for even unsupported versions of Windows to help contain the spread of the ransomware. The WannaCry incident serves as a powerful reminder of the potential consequences of neglecting endpoint security and the importance of proactive measures to prevent similar attacks in the future.

Application Security

Application security refers to the measures and practices designed to protect applications from threats and vulnerabilities throughout their lifecycle. This security discipline aims at ensuring that software applications are secure from design, through development and deployment, to updates and maintenance. It encompasses the hardware, software, processes, and measures that detect or minimize security vulnerabilities.

Importance of Application Security

The significance of application security has grown with the increasing reliance on software applications for critical business operations and personal activities. Applications, whether web-based, mobile, or desktop, are often targeted by attackers due to the valuable data they process and store, including personal information, financial data, and intellectual property. Application security is a critical aspect of overall **Cybersecurity**, addressing the unique risks and challenges associated with software applications. By incorporating security practices throughout the application development lifecycle, organizations can protect against vulnerabilities and threats, ensuring the integrity, confidentiality, and availability of their applications and the data they handle.

Key aspects of application security include:

- Protecting Sensitive Data: Application security helps in safeguarding sensitive information from unauthorized access and data breaches.

- Maintaining Trust: Security incidents can damage an organization's reputation and erode customer trust. Robust application security helps in maintaining user trust and confidence.

- Regulatory Compliance: Many applications are subject to regulatory requirements that mandate stringent data protection and privacy measures. Application security ensures compliance with these regulations, avoiding legal penalties and fines.

- Preventing Financial Losses: Security breaches can lead to significant financial losses, including the costs of remediation, legal fees, and penalties. Application security helps in minimizing these risks.

Components of Application Security
Application security involves various practices and solutions, including:

- Secure Coding Practices: Implementing secure coding guidelines to prevent vulnerabilities such as SQL injection, cross-site scripting (XSS), and buffer overflows. This includes input validation, proper error handling, and the use of security libraries and frameworks.

- Security Testing: Conducting regular security testing at different stages of the application development lifecycle, including static application security testing (SAST), dynamic application security testing (DAST), and penetration testing.

- Authentication and Authorization: Implementing strong authentication and authorization mechanisms to ensure that only legitimate users can access the application and that they can only perform actions permitted to their role.

- Data Encryption: Encrypting sensitive data stored by the application or transmitted over the network to protect it from interception or unauthorized access.

- Dependency Management: Regularly updating and patching third-party libraries and dependencies to protect against vulnerabilities.

- Security Training and Awareness: Educating developers, testers, and relevant staff on secure coding practices and emerging security threats.

- Incident Response: Preparing for potential security incidents with a defined incident response plan that includes procedures for quickly addressing and mitigating vulnerabilities or breaches.

An example of a breach due to application security vulnerabilities is the Equifax breach of 2017. This massive breach compromised the personal information of approximately 147 million people. The attackers exploited a vulnerability in the Apache Struts web application framework used by Equifax's online dispute portal. The specific vulnerability, CVE-2017-5638, was a remote code execution flaw that allowed attackers to gain unauthorized access to Equifax's system.

Despite the availability of a patch for the vulnerability two months prior to the breach, Equifax had not updated its systems with the necessary security patch. This oversight allowed hackers to access and exfiltrate sensitive data, including Social Security numbers, birth dates, addresses, and, in some instances, driver's license numbers and credit card information.

The Equifax breach underscores the critical importance of application security practices such as timely patch management, regular vulnerability assessments, and secure development lifecycle processes. It highlights the potential consequences of failing to address known vulnerabilities in software and web applications, demonstrating the need for organizations to adopt a proactive approach to application security to protect sensitive data from cyber threats.

Data Security

Data security refers to the protective measures and practices implemented to prevent unauthorized access, disclosure, alteration, or destruction of data. It encompasses a broad spectrum of technologies, processes, and controls designed to protect data from various threats, ensuring its confidentiality, integrity, and availability (CIA triad). Data security is critical across all types of data, whether it be personal, financial, intellectual property, or any other sensitive information that an organization or individual might hold. Data security is a critical aspect of an organization's overall **Cybersecurity** posture, as well as an individual's personal data protection strategy. Implementing a comprehensive data security plan that covers all aspects of data protection can help mitigate risks, protect sensitive information, ensure regulatory compliance, and maintain trust with customers and stakeholders. Given the dynamic nature of threats and technology, continuous evaluation and adaptation of data security practices are essential.

Importance of Data Security

The importance of data security is underscored by several factors:

- Privacy Protection: Protecting personal and sensitive information from unauthorized access is crucial to maintaining individuals' privacy rights and compliance with data protection regulations.

- Regulatory Compliance: Organizations are often required to comply with various regulations and standards related to data protection, such as GDPR in Europe, HIPAA in the healthcare sector in the United States, and PCI DSS for payment card information. Effective data security practices help in meeting these regulatory requirements.

- Preventing Data Breaches: Data breaches can result in significant financial losses, legal repercussions, and damage to an organization's reputation. Securing data against breaches is vital for protecting organizational assets and maintaining trust with customers and stakeholders.

- Business Continuity: Ensuring the integrity and availability of data is essential for the continuous operation of business processes. Data security measures help protect against data loss or corruption due to malware, system failures, or disasters.

Components of Data Security
Data security involves a multi-layered approach that includes:

- Access Control: Ensuring that only authorized individuals can access certain data, implementing measures such as authentication, authorization, and identity management.

- Encryption: Using cryptographic methods to convert data into a format that can only be read by someone who has the decryption key, protecting the data at rest, in use, and in transit.

- Data Masking: Anonymizing specific data within a database or application to protect sensitive information while maintaining the data's usability.

- Data Erasure: Securely deleting data when it is no longer needed or when required by compliance regulations, ensuring it cannot be recovered.

- Backup and Recovery: Regularly backing up data and having a robust recovery plan in place to restore data in case of loss or corruption.

- Data Loss Prevention (DLP): Implementing tools and processes to detect potential data breach or data ex-filtration transmissions and prevent them by monitoring, detecting, and blocking sensitive data handling.

- Physical Security: Protecting the physical devices and infrastructure where data is stored and processed, including servers, data centers, and personal computing devices.

Challenges in Data Security

Data security faces several challenges, including the increasing sophistication of cyber threats, the rapid growth of data volumes, the complexity of IT environments, and the constant evolution of technology. Additionally, the human element—such as employee negligence or insider threats—remains one of the biggest vulnerabilities in data security.

One prominent example of a breach resulting from a lack of data security is the 2019 Capital One data breach. In this incident, a hacker gained unauthorized access to the personal information of over 100 million Capital One customers and applicants in the United States, as well as 6 million in Canada. The exposed data included names, addresses, ZIP codes/postal codes, phone numbers, email addresses, dates of birth, and self-reported income. Additionally, 140,000 Social Security numbers of American customers and 80,000 linked bank account numbers of secured credit card customers were compromised.

The breach was primarily due to a misconfigured web application firewall that the attacker, a former Amazon Web Services (AWS) employee, exploited to gain access to the data stored on AWS servers. The attacker utilized a technique known as "server-side request forgery" (SSRF) to trick the firewall into granting unauthorized access to the backend servers where Capital One's data was stored.

This breach highlights several critical aspects of data security that were overlooked, including the importance of proper configuration and management of security tools, regular security assessments to identify and mitigate vulnerabilities, and the need for robust access controls and monitoring to prevent and detect unauthorized access.

The Capital One data breach serves as a cautionary tale about the necessity of comprehensive data security measures, including the secure configuration of services, ongoing vulnerability management, and effective oversight and monitoring of cloud environments and third-party services. It underscores the importance of adhering to best practices in data security to protect sensitive customer information from potential threats.

Identity and Access Management (IAM)

Identity and Access Management (IAM) is a framework of policies and technologies ensuring that the right individuals access the appropriate resources at the right times for the right reasons. IAM systems enable organizations to manage users' identities and their various access permissions to company resources securely and efficiently. This system plays a crucial role in an organization's overall security posture by preventing unauthorized access, data breaches, and allowing for secure and efficient operation. Identity and Access Management is a foundational element of an organization's security strategy, critical for protecting sensitive information and resources in a digital world. By carefully managing who has access to what and ensuring that users are who they claim to be, IAM systems play a vital role in preventing unauthorized access and breaches, all while enhancing efficiency and user experience.

Core Functions of IAM

IAM encompasses several core functions that work together to secure and manage digital identities:

- Authentication: Verifying the identity of a user, device, or system, typically through login credentials, biometric scans, or other methods.

- Authorization: Once authenticated, determining whether the user has permission to access the requested resources based on predefined policies.

- User Management: Creating, managing, and deleting user accounts and identities across systems and applications.

- Role-Based Access Control (RBAC): Assigning and managing access rights based on roles within the organization, ensuring users have access to the information necessary for their roles and nothing beyond that.

- Single Sign-On (SSO): Allowing users to log in once and access multiple systems without needing to re-authenticate, enhancing user convenience and reducing password fatigue.

- Multi-Factor Authentication (MFA): Requiring two or more verification factors to authenticate a user, significantly enhancing security beyond simple password protection.

- Privileged Access Management (PAM): Specifically managing and monitoring access for users with elevated privileges to ensure high-risk operations are protected and audited.

- Identity Federation: Allowing users to access multiple systems and applications across different organizations using a single set of credentials, facilitated by standards like SAML and OAuth.

Importance of IAM
The importance of IAM systems in modern organizations cannot be overstated, with several key benefits driving their adoption:

- Enhanced Security: By ensuring that only authorized users can access resources, IAM helps protect against unauthorized access and potential data breaches.

- Regulatory Compliance: Many regulations require strict control and audit trails over who has access to sensitive information. IAM systems help meet these requirements by providing comprehensive access controls and reporting capabilities.

- Operational Efficiency: Automating the management of user identities, access rights, and authentication processes reduces administrative overhead and improves user productivity.

- Improved User Experience: Features like SSO and MFA improve security while also offering a smoother user experience by minimizing login hassles.

- Flexibility and Scalability: IAM solutions can adapt to changing security needs, easily scaling up as an organization grows or as it adopts new technologies.

Challenges in IAM
While IAM systems provide numerous benefits, they also come with challenges, such as:

- Complexity in Implementation: Deploying an IAM solution across diverse systems and applications can be complex and resource-intensive.

- Balancing Security and Usability: Striking the right balance between strong security measures (like MFA) and not overly burdening users can be challenging.

- Keeping up with Evolving Threats: As **Cybersecurity** threats evolve, IAM systems must continually adapt to new types of attacks and vulnerabilities.

A significant breach that underscores the importance of robust Identity and Access Management (IAM) practices occurred with the Office of Personnel Management (OPM) of the United States in 2015. This cyberattack resulted in the theft of sensitive personal information of approximately 21.5 million individuals, including federal employees, job applicants, and their families. The compromised data included Social Security numbers, names, dates and places of birth, addresses, and fingerprint records. For some individuals, the breach also exposed detailed security clearance information, making the implications particularly severe.

The attackers were able to gain access to OPM's systems by using stolen credentials from a contractor. Once inside the network, they leveraged inadequate access controls to escalate privileges and move laterally across the network, undetected for several months. This breach highlighted multiple failures in IAM, including the insufficient monitoring of third-party access, inadequate use of multi-factor authentication (MFA) for sensitive systems and data, and a lack of effective role-based access controls to limit user access to only what was necessary for their job functions.

This incident illustrates the critical importance of implementing strong IAM policies and technologies, such as enforcing MFA, conducting regular audits and reviews of user access rights, and promptly revoking access for users who no longer require it or whose employment has terminated. Additionally, it emphasizes the need for vigilant monitoring and management of third-party vendor access to ensure that external entities do not become a weak link in the organization's security posture.

The OPM breach serves as a potent reminder of the potential consequences of IAM weaknesses, highlighting the necessity for organizations to adopt a comprehensive approach to identity and access management to safeguard against sophisticated cyber threats.

Incident Response

Incident response is a structured approach to addressing and managing the aftermath of a security breach or cyberattack, also known as an IT incident, computer incident, or security incident. The goal is to handle the situation in a way that limits damage and reduces recovery time and costs. An incident response plan includes a set of written instructions that outline an organization's response to network events, security breaches, and any other types of attacks. Incident response is a crucial component of an organization's security posture, enabling it to respond effectively to security incidents and minimize their impact. Given the inevitability of security incidents in today's digital world, having a well-prepared and practiced incident response team and plan is not just recommended; it's essential for protecting an organization's information, assets, and reputation.

Key Phases of Incident Response

The incident response process can be broken down into several key phases, often described in models like the one developed by the National Institute of Standards and Technology (NIST):

1. Preparation: This foundational phase involves establishing and training an incident response team, developing incident response plans, setting up communication protocols, and preparing tools and technologies to handle potential incidents.

2. Identification: This phase involves detecting and determining the scope of the incident. It includes monitoring security systems for signs of an incident and effectively identifying when an incident has occurred.

3. Containment: Once an incident is identified, the immediate priority is to contain it to prevent further damage. Short-term containment involves stopping the spread of the incident, while

long-term containment aims to temporarily fix the issue until more permanent solutions can be applied.

4. Eradication: After containment, the next step is to remove the cause of the incident and any related malware or attackers from the system. This might involve deleting malicious files, disabling breached user accounts, or updating security vulnerabilities.

5. Recovery: In this phase, affected systems and devices are restored and returned to the operational environment. Recovery actions can include restoring systems from clean backups, reinstalling operating systems, and applying patches.

6. Lessons Learned: Perhaps the most critical phase, this involves analyzing the incident and the response to identify what was done well and what could be improved. This review should take place shortly after the incident and might include documenting changes to policies or procedures, security measures to prevent future incidents, and conducting follow-up monitoring to ensure systems are not re-compromised.

Importance of Incident Response
Effective incident response is critical for several reasons:

- Minimizing Damage: Quick and effective response can significantly reduce the damage caused by security incidents, including financial losses, data breaches, and loss of reputation.

- Reducing Recovery Time and Costs: A well-executed incident response can shorten the recovery time from security incidents, thereby reducing the associated costs.

- Compliance: Many industries are regulated by laws and standards that require an incident response plan. Non-compliance can result in fines and legal penalties.

- Maintaining Trust: Demonstrating an ability to quickly and effectively deal with security incidents helps maintain the trust of customers, partners, and stakeholders.

A clear example of a breach exacerbated by insufficient incident response is the Equifax breach in 2017. While the initial breach was due to an unpatched vulnerability in the Apache Struts web framework, the aftermath highlighted significant failures in Equifax's incident response.

After discovering the breach, Equifax's response was criticized for multiple reasons:

1. Delayed Disclosure: Equifax waited six weeks to publicly disclose the breach after discovering it, affecting approximately 147 million people. This delay hindered the affected individuals' ability to take prompt action to protect themselves from potential identity theft and fraud.

2. Inadequate Communication: When Equifax did disclose the breach, their communication was seen as insufficient and unclear. The information provided to the public was not comprehensive, and their instructions on how affected individuals could protect themselves were criticized for being vague and confusing.

3. Faulty Support Systems: In response to the breach, Equifax set up a dedicated website for affected individuals to check if they were impacted and to sign up for credit monitoring. However, the site was plagued with issues, including security warnings from browsers, vulnerability to spoofing, and initially, ambiguous terms of service that suggested users might be waiving their rights to sue Equifax if they used the service.

4. Unprepared Customer Service: Equifax's customer service was overwhelmed, with many reporting that representatives were unable to provide clear information or assistance. This lack of preparation for handling inquiries further eroded public trust.

The Equifax incident underscores the importance of a well-prepared and executed incident response plan that includes not only the technical means to address and mitigate a breach but also clear, timely communication and support for those affected. Effective incident response plans should be comprehensive, encompassing not just the immediate technical response but also how to communicate with stakeholders, manage public relations, and provide support to mitigate the impact on customers or users. This incident demonstrates how crucial a robust, practiced incident response strategy is to managing the fallout from a breach and maintaining or restoring trust among users and the public.

User Education and Awareness

User education and awareness are critical components of an organization's **Cybersecurity** strategy, playing a pivotal role in safeguarding against a wide array of cyber threats. Human error is often cited as one of the weakest links in the **Cybersecurity** chain, with social engineering attacks like phishing exploiting this vulnerability. By investing in user education and awareness programs, organizations can significantly enhance their overall security posture.

Importance of User Education and Awareness

Mitigating Human Error: Many security breaches are the result of human error. Educating users on recognizing and responding to cyber threats can drastically reduce the likelihood of incidents caused by mistaken actions or oversights.

Empowering Users: Knowledgeable users can act as a first line of defense against cyber threats. By understanding potential risks and the importance of their actions, users are more likely to adhere to security policies and practices.

Adapting to Evolving Threats: Cyber threats are constantly evolving, with attackers continuously developing new techniques. Regular training ensures that users are up-to-date on the latest threats and how to avoid them.

Enhancing Compliance: Many regulatory frameworks require ongoing user training as part of compliance. Regular education sessions can ensure that organizations meet these requirements, avoiding potential fines and penalties.

Protecting Brand Reputation: Security incidents can damage an organization's reputation. By preventing breaches through user education, organizations can protect their brand integrity and customer trust.

Large Data Breaches Due to Phishing

Phishing attacks have been at the heart of several high-profile data breaches, demonstrating the critical need for user education and awareness. Phishing involves deceiving individuals into providing sensitive information or clicking on malicious links by masquerading as a trustworthy entity in digital communication.

- Anthem Inc.: In 2015, the second-largest health insurer in the U.S. experienced a massive data breach affecting 78.8 million records. Attackers gained access to personal information through a sophisticated phishing attack targeting Anthem's employees.

- Sony Pictures: In 2014, Sony Pictures suffered a significant breach where attackers used phishing emails to gain access to the company's network, leading to the leak of sensitive data, personal information of employees, and unreleased films.

- Ubiquiti Networks: In 2015, this manufacturer of networking technology for service providers and enterprises lost $46.7 million to a phishing scam where attackers impersonated communications from executive management, requesting fund transfers.

These incidents highlight the importance of training users to recognize and respond appropriately to phishing and other social engineering attacks. Regular, engaging, and comprehensive education and awareness programs can equip users with the knowledge to act as an effective human firewall, significantly reducing the risk of data breaches and enhancing an organization's security posture.

Key Security Models or Standards

After spending over two decades in the cybersecurity field, I've come to appreciate the critical importance of familiarizing oneself with foundational models and standards. Among these, the Zero Trust Security Model is particularly noteworthy for its core premise: assume the presence of threats both inside and outside the network. This approach emphasizes the necessity of verifying every access request, regardless of origin, truly embodying the 'never trust, always verify' principle.

An understanding of the OSI model is equally essential, as it clarifies the various layers of network communication. Grasping this model is crucial because the security measures and equipment we choose may function primarily at specific layers, directly influencing our strategies for protecting network communications.

I consider the CIS 18 (formerly known as CIS 20) another foundational standard, especially when taking over security for a new company that hasn't undergone an audit before. It provides a comprehensive framework for assessing security from a technical perspective, acting as an excellent initial step towards a more thorough review in line with the National Institute of Standards and Technology (NIST) guidelines.

Moreover, ISO/IEC 27001 warrants attention for its international acclaim as a benchmark in information security management. This standard outlines a holistic framework for establishing, implementing, and maintaining an information security management system (ISMS), presenting a structured method for safeguarding and managing information globally.

To conclude this section, the importance of secure coding practices cannot be overstated. The security and integrity of an organization's digital infrastructure hinge on the quality of the underlying code. Thus, adopting secure coding standards is crucial for reducing vulnerabilities and enhancing the resilience of software applications against cyber threats.

Zero Trust Security Model

The Zero Trust Security Model is a **Cybersecurity** strategy that operates on a fundamental principle: trust no one and verify everything. This approach assumes that threats can exist both outside and inside the network, thus, no users or devices should be automatically trusted, regardless of their location relative to the network perimeter. Instead, every attempt to access a system or data must be authenticated, authorized, and continuously validated for security compliance with the organization's policies, before access is granted or maintained.

Key Concepts of the Zero Trust Security Model include:
Least Privilege Access: Users and devices are given the minimum level of access — or privileges — needed to perform their functions. This limits the potential damage from breaches or insider threats.

Microsegmentation: The network is divided into small, secure zones. Access to these zones requires separate authentication, making it harder for an attacker to move laterally across a network.

Multi-Factor Authentication (MFA): Requires more than one piece of evidence to authenticate a user; this could include something the user knows (password), something the user has (security token), and something the user is (biometric verification).

Continuous Monitoring and Validation: The security posture of users and devices is continuously checked to ensure compliance with security policies. Access can be revoked at any time if anomalies or changes in context are detected.

Explicit Verification: No entity, whether a user, device, or network system, is trusted by default from inside or outside the network.

Verification is required from everyone trying to access resources on the network.

Implementation Considerations

Implementing a Zero Trust security model involves a fundamental shift in how organizations approach their network and security architectures. It's a move away from traditional security models that assume everything inside the network is safe. Instead, Zero Trust operates under the principle of "never trust, always verify," treating all users and devices—both inside and outside the network—as potential threats. Here are key considerations for successfully implementing a Zero Trust model:

1. Identify Sensitive Data and Assets
- Asset Discovery: Begin by identifying and classifying all assets within your organization, including data, devices, applications, and services. Understanding what needs to be protected is critical.

- Data Classification: Classify data based on sensitivity and compliance requirements to ensure appropriate protection levels are applied.

2. Map the Transaction Flows
- Understand Communication Paths: Map how traffic moves across your network, focusing on how data and services interact. This understanding is crucial for implementing precise access controls and monitoring.

3. Architect a Zero Trust Network
- Microsegmentation: Divide the network into smaller, isolated segments to limit lateral movement and provide tailored security policies based on the sensitivity of the data in each segment.

- Least-Privilege Access: Implement strict access controls that give users and devices the minimum level of access needed to perform their functions.

4. Implement Multi-factor Authentication (MFA)
- Strong Authentication: Ensure that all users, both internal and external, authenticate using multiple factors before granting access to resources. This is a cornerstone of the Zero Trust model.

5. Apply Zero Trust Principles to All Network Layers
- Layered Security: Apply Zero Trust principles not just to data and applications but also to the network, infrastructure, and endpoints. This includes encrypting data at rest and in transit, securing endpoints, and protecting the infrastructure.

6. Monitor and Enforce Policies
- Continuous Monitoring: Implement tools and processes for real-time monitoring and logging of network activity. This helps in detecting and responding to threats promptly.

- Security Policy Enforcement: Use automated tools to enforce security policies dynamically based on the continuous assessment of trust and risk.

7. Embrace Security Automation and Orchestration
- Automated Response: Utilize security automation and orchestration tools to respond to threats swiftly. Automation can help in dynamically adjusting access controls and security policies based on detected risks.

8. Educate and Train Stakeholders
- Awareness and Training: Educate employees, contractors, and partners about the Zero Trust model, including the importance of security practices such as using MFA and recognizing phishing attempts.

9. Select and Integrate the Right Technologies
- Technology Selection: Choose security solutions that can integrate well with each other and support the enforcement of Zero Trust principles.

- Vendor Assessment: Assess vendors on their ability to support Zero Trust architectures, including their security features, integration capabilities, and compliance with industry standards.

10. Review and Adjust Regularly
- Continuous Improvement: Regularly review and adjust security policies, controls, and technologies to adapt to new threats, organizational changes, and technological advancements.

Implementing Zero Trust is a complex process that requires careful planning and execution. Organizations should approach implementation as an ongoing journey, continually evolving their security posture to adapt to the changing threat landscape and organizational needs.

Benefits of Zero Trust
Enhanced Security Posture: By assuming that threats could be anywhere and reinforcing security checks, Zero Trust significantly reduces the risk of data breaches and insider threats.

Improved Compliance and Data Protection: Continuous verification helps ensure that data access is appropriately controlled, aiding compliance with regulations like GDPR, HIPAA, etc.

Adaptability to Modern Work Environments: Zero Trust accommodates remote work, BYOD (Bring Your Own Device), and cloud-based resources, reflecting the needs of modern, dynamic work environments.

Zero Trust is not a product but a comprehensive approach to network security that requires strategic planning, proper implementation, and ongoing management. It's an evolving security model designed to cope with the sophisticated and constantly changing threat landscape in today's digital world.

OSI Model (Open Systems Interconnection)

The OSI (Open Systems Interconnection) model is a conceptual framework used to understand and standardize the functions of a telecommunication or computing system without regard to its underlying internal structure and technology. Developed by the International Organization for Standardization (ISO) in 1978, the OSI model divides the tasks involved with moving data from one computing system to another into seven distinct layers. Each layer serves a specific function and communicates with the layers directly above and below it. From top to bottom, the seven layers are:

Application Layer (Layer 7):
The closest layer to the end user, which interacts with software applications to implement a communicating component. This layer provides services such as email, file transfer, and other data exchange for programs running on a computer.

Presentation Layer (Layer 6):
Translates data between the application layer and the network. It's responsible for data encryption/decryption, compression/decompression, and translation of data from one format to another.

Session Layer (Layer 5):
Establishes, manages, and terminates connections between applications. It's responsible for setting up, coordinating, and terminating conversations, exchanges, and dialogs between the applications at each end.

Transport Layer (Layer 4):
Provides reliable data transfer across a network, including error checking and recovery, as well as flow control. Protocols like TCP (Transmission Control Protocol) and UDP (User Datagram Protocol) operate at this layer.

Network Layer (Layer 3):
Handles routing of data across networks and ensures that data gets from its source to its destination by determining the best path. It manages packet addressing and forwarding. The Internet Protocol (IP) is a key protocol that operates at this layer.

Data Link Layer (Layer 2):
Responsible for node-to-node data transfer and error detection and handling. It provides the means to transfer data between network entities and might address issues like frame synchronization, flow control, and error notification. Ethernet and Wi-Fi are examples of protocols that work at this layer.

Physical Layer (Layer 1):
Concerns with the physical transmission of data, including how bits are signaled by hardware devices that directly interface with a network medium, such as cables and switches. This layer defines the electrical, mechanical, procedural, and functional specifications for activating, maintaining, and deactivating the physical link between communicating network systems.

The OSI model is an essential tool for teaching and understanding how different networking technologies work together to move data from one system to another. It helps in troubleshooting network problems by enabling network administrators to isolate issues to a specific layer of the model.

Center for Internet Security (CIS) Controls

The CIS Controls are a prioritized set of actions that help protect organizations and their data from known cyber-attack vectors. The CIS Controls have evolved over time, and as of my last update, the most recent version is organized into a set of 18 critical security controls. These controls are designed to provide an actionable guide for securing information systems and data. The list is updated periodically to reflect the changing nature of cyber threats and the latest best practices in cybersecurity.

Here's an overview of the CIS 18, breaking down each control and its primary focus:

1. Inventory and Control of Hardware Assets: Maintain an up-to-date inventory of all hardware devices to ensure only authorized devices are connected to the network.

2. Inventory and Control of Software Assets: Keep an inventory of software assets to enable the management of software on the network and ensure that only authorized software is installed and used.

3. Continuous Vulnerability Management: Regularly scan and remediate vulnerabilities in a timely manner to minimize the window of opportunity for attackers.

4. Controlled Use of Administrative Privileges: Manage and control administrative privileges to reduce the chances of misuse or malicious use of elevated rights.

5. Secure Configuration for Hardware and Software: Establish, implement, and actively manage security configurations for all hardware and software to reduce vulnerabilities and maintain a secure state.

6. Maintenance, Monitoring, and Analysis of Audit Logs: Collect, manage, and analyze audit logs to detect unauthorized access or anomalous activity, and to support forensic investigations.

7. Email and Web Browser Protections: Implement measures to secure email and web browsing activities, which are common attack vectors.

8. Malware Defenses: Deploy and maintain anti-malware defenses across the organization to detect and prevent the spread of malware.

9. Limitation and Control of Network Ports, Protocols, and Services: Manage the use of network ports, protocols, and services on devices, minimizing windows of vulnerability.

10. Data Recovery Capabilities: Ensure that data can be recovered in the event of loss or damage through regular backups and recovery procedures.

11. Secure Configuration of Network Devices: Implement secure configurations for network devices such as firewalls, routers, and switches to protect against attacks.

12. Boundary Defense: Detect, prevent, and correct the flow of information transferring networks of different trust levels with a focus on security-damaging data.

13. Data Protection: Protect sensitive data through encryption, access controls, and data policies to prevent unauthorized access and data exfiltration.

14. Controlled Access Based on the Need to Know: Enforce access controls and information flow control policies based on users' need to know sensitive information.

15. Wireless Access Control: Secure wireless network access to protect against unauthorized access and eavesdropping.

16. Account Monitoring and Control: Actively manage the life cycle of user accounts, including creation, use, and removal, to reduce the risk of unauthorized access.

17. Implement a Security Awareness and Training Program: Educate employees about cybersecurity threats and safe practices to reduce the risk of human error.

18. Application Software Security: Ensure that applications are secure to protect against vulnerabilities and attacks that target application flaws.

These controls are widely regarded as effective measures for reducing the risk of cyber threats. Organizations are encouraged to implement these controls not just in isolation but as part of a comprehensive, layered cybersecurity strategy. It's important to note that while the CIS Controls provide a strong foundation for security, they should be adapted and prioritized based on the specific needs and risk profile of each organization.

NIST

The National Institute of Standards and Technology (NIST) is a non-regulatory agency of the United States Department of Commerce. NIST's role encompasses a wide range of activities aimed at promoting innovation and industrial competitiveness across various industries through measurement science, standards, and technology in ways that enhance economic security and improve quality of life.

Key Functions and Contributions of NIST:

1. Development of Standards and Guidelines: NIST develops standards and guidelines to help ensure the reliability and security of information systems and technology. This includes foundational benchmarks for cybersecurity practices, data encryption, and privacy controls, among other areas.

2. Research and Innovation: NIST conducts research in various fields of science and technology, including materials science, engineering, information technology, and quantum science. This research supports the advancement of technology and innovation.

3. Measurement Science: NIST plays a critical role in developing measurement standards that support scientific research, commerce, and manufacturing. This includes everything from the calibration of weights and measures to the standards for time and the spectrum.

4. Promoting Industrial Competitiveness: By providing technical support, tools, and partnerships, NIST aids U.S. industries in improving their competitiveness in the global marketplace. This includes helping small and medium-sized businesses with cybersecurity and other technological challenges.

NIST and Cybersecurity:
NIST's contributions to cybersecurity are significant and widely recognized. Some of the key cybersecurity frameworks, guidelines, and standards developed by NIST include:

- NIST Cybersecurity Framework (CSF): Provides a policy framework of computer security guidance for how private sector organizations in the US can assess and improve their ability to prevent, detect, and respond to cyber-attacks. It's widely used by organizations of all sizes and industries to manage and mitigate cybersecurity risk.

- Special Publication 800 Series (NIST SP 800): A series of publications that provide comprehensive guidelines, recommendations, and best practices for federal information systems, including detailed information on cybersecurity topics such as risk management, cloud computing security, and identity and access management.

- Federal Information Processing Standards (FIPS): Publicly announced standards developed by the United States federal government for use in computer systems by non-military government agencies and government contractors. FIPS standards cover topics such as encryption algorithms and protocols.

NIST's work is instrumental in setting the baseline for security and privacy that influences global standards and practices. Whether it's through developing cybersecurity frameworks, conducting cutting-edge research, or establishing measurement standards, NIST's contributions continue to play a crucial role in shaping the technological landscape.

ISO/IEC 27001

ISO/IEC 27001 is an internationally recognized standard for managing information security. Published by the International Organization for Standardization (ISO) and the International Electrotechnical Commission (IEC), it specifies the requirements for establishing, implementing, maintaining, and continually improving an information security management system (ISMS). The standard is designed to help organizations secure their information assets and manage the security of assets such as financial information, intellectual property, employee details, and information entrusted by third parties.

Key Components of ISO/IEC 27001:
- ISMS: At the heart of ISO/IEC 27001 is the requirement to establish an ISMS, a systematic approach consisting of processes, technology, and people that helps you protect and manage your organization's information through effective risk management.

- Risk Management: Central to the standard is the assessment and treatment of information security risks. Organizations are required to identify potential information security risks and then define control objectives and controls to manage or reduce these risks.

- Control Objectives and Controls: The standard includes a set of control objectives and controls (previously known as Annex A), which are guidelines and best practices for implementing effective information security measures. These controls are selected based on the risk assessment process and can be customized to fit the specific needs of the organization.

- Continuous Improvement: ISO/IEC 27001 emphasizes the importance of continual improvement through regular reviews and updates to the ISMS, ensuring that it evolves to meet changing risks and business needs.

Benefits of ISO/IEC 27001 Certification:
- Enhanced Security: Implementing an ISMS according to ISO/IEC 27001 standards helps protect an organization's information from security breaches, data leaks, and other threats.

- Increased Credibility and Trust: Certification can demonstrate to customers, partners, and stakeholders that the organization is committed to managing information securely, thereby enhancing business relationships and customer confidence.

- Compliance: Helps in meeting legal, regulatory, and contractual obligations regarding information security, privacy, and IT governance.

- Competitive Advantage: Certification can provide a competitive edge in the marketplace, particularly when sensitive data handling and security are critical for business operations.

- Risk Management: Provides a systematic framework for identifying and managing risks to the security of information.

Process of Certification:
Achieving ISO/IEC 27001 certification involves a multi-step process, including:

1. Planning and Scope Definition: Defining the scope of the ISMS, identifying relevant stakeholders, and establishing the ISMS policy.

2. Risk Assessment: Conducting a comprehensive risk assessment to identify and evaluate information security risks.

3. Implementing Controls: Implementing the necessary controls to mitigate identified risks and achieve the control objectives.

4. Internal Audit: Conducting an internal audit to evaluate the ISMS against the ISO/IEC 27001 requirements.

5. Management Review: Reviewing the performance and effectiveness of the ISMS at the management level.

6. Certification Audit: Undergoing an external audit performed by an accredited certification body. If successful, the organization is awarded the ISO/IEC 27001 certification.

Maintaining certification requires regular surveillance audits and a three-year recertification audit, ensuring that the ISMS continues to operate according to the standard's requirements.

ISO/IEC 27001 offers a robust framework for managing information security, providing a systematic approach to minimizing information security risks and ensuring business continuity. Organizations that have met this certification will typically gain more trust from customers due to the understanding that their environment has been tested and confirmed as secure. As of recently this standard was updated in 2022.

Secure Coding

Secure coding refers to the practice of writing computer software in a way that guards against the introduction of security vulnerabilities. It involves applying a series of guidelines and techniques to improve the security of code, making it more resistant to attacks and breaches. The goal is to ensure that software is as free from vulnerabilities as possible, not only in its initial development but also through its entire lifecycle.

Secure coding practices encompass a wide range of topics, including but not limited to:

Input Validation:

Ensuring that all input received from users, systems, or external devices is validated before being processed to prevent injection attacks, such as SQL injection or cross-site scripting (XSS).

Authentication and Authorization:

Implementing strong authentication and authorization mechanisms to ensure that users are who they claim to be and have the correct permissions to access resources.

Cryptography:

Using cryptography correctly to protect data in transit and at rest, including the proper selection and implementation of encryption algorithms.

Error Handling:

 Safely managing errors so that they do not leak sensitive information or create opportunities for exploitation.

Session Management:

Securing user sessions to protect against attacks like session hijacking or fixation.

Dependency Management:
Ensuring that third-party libraries and dependencies are up-to-date, free from known vulnerabilities, and securely configured.

Resources on Secure Coding

NIST (National Institute of Standards and Technology):
NIST publishes a vast array of guidelines that cover different aspects of **Cybersecurity**, including secure coding practices. Their publications can be accessed through their website, and specific documents like the "NIST Special Publication 800-53" provide guidelines for security and privacy controls for federal information systems and organizations, including aspects of secure coding.

SEI CERT Coding Standards:
The SEI's Computer Emergency Response Team (CERT) offers coding standards aimed at preventing software vulnerabilities. These standards cover various programming languages and provide detailed guidelines for secure coding practices. The CERT Coding Standards can be found on the SEI website and are widely respected in both government and industry sectors for their comprehensiveness and practicality.

These resources offer guidelines and best practices that are beneficial for developers looking to enhance the security of their software through secure coding practices.

In the early stages of my career, I was privileged to work as a software developer on projects that were deployed globally, at a time when the concept of secure coding was not yet a widely recognized or implemented standard across the industry. During a routine examination of our software, I uncovered a significant oversight in a specific segment of our codebase. Although we had implemented stringent security measures across most of our software, this particular section lacked the necessary authentication mechanisms due to an initial design flaw. This gap in security presented a potential risk, as it could have allowed unauthorized individuals to gain control over remote machines running our software. The discovery of this vulnerability was a pivotal moment for me, highlighting the critical need for comprehensive security protocols in all phases of software development. It profoundly influenced my approach to programming, instilling a deep commitment to integrating rigorous security and authentication measures. Had this vulnerability been exploited before we identified and rectified it, attackers would have had the capability to commandeer any server hosting our software, posing a severe threat to our users' security.

Explanation of other Technologies

With over two decades of experience in the field, I have identified several critical areas within cybersecurity that demand ongoing attention and in-depth understanding. These areas have been pivotal in my work, encompassing both ethical hacking to fortify organizational security defenses and the analysis of their application in real-world attacks. Moreover, my proficiency extends to leveraging software tools related to these topics, enabling me to effectively counteract cyber threats. Given the rapid technological advancements and the emergence of artificial intelligence, the repertoire of tools available for cybersecurity is expected to grow significantly. This blend of offensive and defensive tactics, along with an ever-expanding toolkit, highlights the critical importance of staying abreast of developments in this fast-evolving domain of cybersecurity

Security Information and Event Management (SEIM)

SIEM is a significant field in **Cybersecurity**, providing a holistic view of an organization's information security. SIEM systems work by collecting and aggregating log data generated throughout the organization's technology infrastructure, from host systems and applications to network and security devices such as firewalls and antivirus filters.

Here's a brief overview of what SIEM offers:

Log Collection and Management:
SIEM systems collect and store log data from various sources within an organization's infrastructure, making it easier for security analysts to search through a centralized repository of information.

Event Correlation:
These systems correlate events from different sources to identify patterns of activity that might indicate a security threat or a compliance issue.

Alerting and Reporting: SIEM provides real-time analysis of security alerts generated by applications and network hardware. It can prioritize alerts based on the severity of the threat, helping analysts to focus on the most critical issues first.

Forensic Analysis:
In the aftermath of a security incident, SIEM systems can help in forensic analysis by providing detailed log information that can be used to understand what happened, how the attack was carried out, and which systems were affected.

Compliance Management:
Many SIEM solutions come with built-in support for compliance reporting for various standards and regulations, making it easier for organizations to meet their compliance requirements.

The main goal of SIEM is to offer a comprehensive overview of an organization's security posture, enabling rapid detection, analysis, and response to potential security threats.

Anti-virus

Anti-virus software is a category of programs designed to prevent, search for, detect, and remove software viruses, and other malicious software like worms, trojans, adware, and more. These tools are a critical component of computer and internet security, especially for users who may encounter malware in email attachments, downloaded files, or through malicious websites.

How Anti-virus Software Works

Anti-virus software typically uses a combination of detection methods:

- Signature-based Detection: This is the most common method. The anti-virus software checks a file against a database of known malware signatures — unique strings of data or characteristics that are indicative of malicious software. Because this method relies on known signatures, it's crucial for the anti-virus databases to be regularly updated to recognize new malware.

- Heuristic-based Detection: This method is used to identify new malware or variants of known malware by examining the behavior and characteristics of files. Heuristic analysis can detect malware that hasn't yet been discovered or has been modified and is not yet included in signature databases.

- Behavioral-based Detection: Also known as behavior monitoring, this technique observes the behavior of programs in real-time. If a piece of software acts similarly to known malware after it has been executed, the anti-virus software can take action to stop it, often quarantining the file and alerting the user.

- Sandbox Detection: Some advanced anti-virus programs use this method to execute suspicious programs in a virtual environment (a "sandbox"). This allows the anti-virus to analyze the behavior of the program without risking the actual system's security.

- Data Mining Techniques: Modern anti-virus solutions may also employ data mining and machine learning algorithms to predict and identify malware based on file features and patterns.

Features of Anti-virus Software

Beyond malware detection and removal, anti-virus software often includes additional features such as:

- Real-time scanning: Monitoring the system for malware and security threats in real-time.

- Automatic updates: Regularly updating malware definitions and software modules to combat new threats.

- Heuristic analysis: Enhancing detection capabilities for new, modified, or previously unknown threats.

- System scans: Offering full system scans, quick scans of critical areas, and custom scans as per user requirements.

- Quarantine and removal: Isolating suspicious files and providing options for their removal or restoration.

- Email scanning: Scanning incoming and outgoing emails and their attachments for malware.

- Web protection: Blocking malicious websites and downloads.

- Firewall integration: Preventing unauthorized access to a computer system through network monitoring.

Choosing and Using Anti-virus Software

When selecting anti-virus software, consider factors like detection rates, system resource usage, user interface friendliness, and the availability of technical support. Regardless of which anti-virus software is used, the following practices can enhance protection:

- Regular Updates: Keep your anti-virus software and its malware signature database up to date.

- Scheduled Scans: Regularly schedule full system scans, especially if real-time scanning is not enabled.

- Safe Computing Practices: Use strong, unique passwords, be cautious with email attachments and downloads, and avoid clicking on suspicious links.

- Keep Software Updated: Ensure your operating system and all applications are kept up to date with the latest patches and updates to minimize vulnerabilities.

Anti-virus software plays a crucial role in the **Cybersecurity** ecosystem, offering a foundational layer of defense against a wide array of threats. However, it should be part of a broader security strategy that includes firewalls, anti-spyware, and safe computing practices to provide comprehensive protection against evolving digital threats.

DLP

Data Loss Prevention (DLP) refers to strategies and solutions aimed at preventing unauthorized access to, or disclosure of, sensitive information. This includes a broad range of data protection techniques and technologies designed to detect and prevent the potential leakage or misuse of data while ensuring its confidentiality, integrity, and availability. DLP solutions are crucial for organizations to comply with privacy laws and regulations, protect intellectual property, and prevent financial loss or damage to reputation stemming from data breaches.

Key Components of DLP

DLP strategies encompass a variety of methods and tools, each tailored to protect data at different stages of its lifecycle: at rest (stored data), in use (data being processed), and in motion (data being transmitted over a network). Effective DLP involves:

- Content Inspection and Contextual Analysis: Analyzing data to identify sensitive or confidential information based on predefined policies or regulations, such as personally identifiable information (PII), financial information, or health records.

- Network Traffic Monitoring: Monitoring data in motion to detect and prevent unauthorized data transfers across network boundaries.

- Endpoint Protection: Controlling data transfer activities on endpoints (e.g., laptops, mobile devices) to prevent data from being moved to unauthorized devices or removable storage.

- Storage Discovery: Identifying where sensitive data is stored across the organization's infrastructure, including cloud storage and remote servers, to ensure it is adequately protected.

Implementing DLP Solutions

The implementation of DLP solutions involves several key steps:

1. Data Identification: The first step is to identify the types of data that need to be protected. This could include a wide range of sensitive or regulated data types.

2. Policy Creation: Based on the identified data, organizations create policies that define what constitutes sensitive data, how it should be handled, and what controls are required to protect it. These policies are then enforced by DLP solutions.

3. Deployment: DLP solutions can be deployed on endpoints, network appliances, or integrated into storage systems and cloud services to monitor and protect data wherever it resides.

4. Monitoring and Blocking: DLP tools continuously monitor data operations and user activities. If a potential data leak is detected, the solution can alert administrators, block the transaction, or quarantine the data, depending on the severity and the configured response actions.

5. Incident Response and Reporting: In the event of a policy violation, DLP solutions provide detailed reporting and analysis tools to help organizations respond to incidents and comply with regulatory reporting requirements.

Challenges and Considerations

While DLP solutions are an essential component of data security, implementing them effectively can present challenges:

- Complexity and Overhead: DLP solutions can be complex to configure and manage, requiring ongoing effort to refine policies and minimize false positives.

- User Impact: Strict DLP policies can sometimes interfere with legitimate business processes, leading to user frustration. Balancing security with usability is crucial.

- Evolving Data Landscapes: As organizations adopt new technologies and data storage solutions, DLP strategies must evolve to cover new data types and communication channels.

IP Scanning

Scanning IP addresses for vulnerabilities is a crucial aspect of **Cybersecurity**, enabling organizations and security professionals to identify potential weaknesses in their networks before they are exploited by malicious actors. This short blog will introduce the basics of vulnerability scanning, cover some common tools and techniques, and provide best practices to ensure effective and ethical scanning.

Understanding Vulnerability Scanning

Vulnerability scanning is the process of automatically reviewing a system or network to identify security weaknesses. These scans can detect vulnerabilities such as unpatched software, insecure configurations, and open ports that could be exploited by hackers. By identifying these vulnerabilities early, organizations can take preemptive action to secure their systems.

Tools and Techniques

Several tools and techniques are used in vulnerability scanning, ranging from simple port scanners to comprehensive vulnerability assessment tools. Here are a few popular ones:

Nmap: A powerful and versatile tool for network discovery and security auditing. Nmap can identify devices on a network, discover open ports, and even determine what software and version are running on the target system.

OpenVAS: A full-featured vulnerability scanner that can detect thousands of vulnerabilities in network services and software.

Nessus: A widely used vulnerability scanner known for its comprehensive database of vulnerabilities and user-friendly interface.

Best Practices for Effective Scanning
To ensure that vulnerability scanning is both effective and ethical, consider the following best practices:

Obtain Permission: Always get explicit permission before scanning networks or systems you do not own. Unauthorized scanning can be illegal and considered hostile by the target.

Define the Scope: Clearly define what systems and networks will be scanned to avoid any unintended consequences, such as disrupting critical services.

Schedule Scans: Appropriately: Schedule scans during off-peak hours to minimize the impact on network performance and avoid disrupting business operations.

Review and Act on Findings: Simply identifying vulnerabilities is not enough. It's crucial to review the findings, prioritize them based on risk, and take appropriate action to mitigate or eliminate the vulnerabilities.

Continuous Monitoring: Regularly scan your systems and networks for vulnerabilities, as new vulnerabilities are constantly being discovered, and your environment may change over time.

Ethical Considerations
Vulnerability scanning can be a double-edged sword. While it's a powerful method for improving security, it can also be misused. Ethical considerations must be taken into account to ensure that scanning activities do not harm or disrupt the target systems. Additionally, the information obtained from scans should be handled with care, ensuring that it does not fall into the wrong hands.

Nmap

Nmap, short for Network Mapper, is an open-source tool for network exploration and security auditing. It was designed to rapidly scan large networks, although it works fine against single hosts. Nmap is widely used by **Cybersecurity** professionals and network administrators to discover devices running on their networks, identify open ports, detect service versions, and find vulnerabilities. Here's a detailed look at Nmap and how to use it effectively.

Nmap is available for various platforms, including Windows, Linux, and macOS. You can download it from the [official Nmap website] (https://nmap.org/download.html). Installation is straightforward, following the instructions specific to your operating system.

Basic Scans

Once installed, Nmap can be run from the command line (terminal in Linux/macOS, Command Prompt or PowerShell in Windows). Here are some basic commands to get you started:

Scan a Single IP Address: To scan a specific IP address, use the command `nmap <IP address>`. For example, `nmap 192.168.1.1` will scan the host with that IP address.

Scan a Range of IP Addresses: You can also scan a range of IP addresses by using a command like `nmap 192.168.1.1-20` to scan hosts from 192.168.1.1 to 192.168.1.20.

Scan an Entire Subnet: To scan every device on a subnet, use the command `nmap 192.168.1.0/24`. This will scan 256 IP addresses from 192.168.1.0 to 192.168.1.255.

Advanced Scanning Options

Nmap offers a wide range of options for more detailed scanning:

Port Scanning: By default, Nmap scans the 1,000 most common ports. You can specify a specific port with `nmap -p <port number> <IP address>` or a range of ports with `nmap -p <start port>-<end port> <IP address>`.

Scan Types: Nmap allows for different types of scans, such as TCP SYN scan (`-sS`), TCP connect scan (`-sT`), UDP scan (`-sU`), and more. Each scan type is suitable for different scenarios and provides different levels of stealth and speed.

Version Detection: Use the `-sV` option to attempt to determine the version of the services running on open ports.

Operating System Detection: The `-O` option enables Nmap to use a series of TCP/IP stack fingerprinting methods to guess the operating system of the target host.

Script Scanning: Nmap's Scripting Engine (`-sC`) allows for the execution of scripts for more advanced discovery and exploitation. It's a powerful feature for vulnerability scanning and network discovery.

Best Practices and Tips

Run Nmap as an Administrator or Root: Some of Nmap's features, like raw packet scans, require root privileges or administrator access.

- Be Ethical and Legal: Only scan networks and systems you own or have explicit permission to scan. Unauthorized scanning can be considered illegal or hostile.

- Start with a Ping Scan: Before conducting a full scan, you might want to do a simple ping scan (`nmap -sn <target>`) to see which hosts are up.

- Be Stealthy: If you're conducting a security audit, use stealthier scan types like the SYN scan to avoid detection by simple intrusion detection systems.

- Read the Nmap Documentation: Nmap has extensive documentation and a very helpful manual. Use the command `man nmap` or visit the [Nmap documentation](https://nmap.org/docs.html) online to explore all its capabilities.

OpenVAS

OpenVAS, now known as GVM (Greenbone Vulnerability Management), is a comprehensive vulnerability scanning and vulnerability management solution. It's an open-source framework consisting of several services and tools to provide a powerful and full-featured vulnerability scanning and vulnerability management experience. GVM is developed and maintained by Greenbone Networks, and it's the open-source version of their commercial product. The suite offers a robust set of features for scanning network devices, systems, and applications to identify vulnerabilities, along with tools for managing and analyzing the results.

Components of GVM

GVM consists of several key components that work together to provide comprehensive vulnerability management:

- Greenbone Vulnerability Manager (gvmd): The central management service that handles user management, feed management, and the database.

- Greenbone Security Assistant (GSA): The web-based GUI that allows users to manage scans, view reports, and configure settings.

- OpenVAS Scanner (openvassd): The component that actually performs the scans, testing targets for thousands of vulnerabilities.

- GVM Libraries (gvm-libs): Libraries shared by all the GVM components.

- Greenbone Security Feed (GSF): A collection of vulnerability tests (VTs), updated daily, that the scanner uses to identify vulnerabilities.

Setting Up GVM

The setup process for GVM can vary depending on the operating system and the specific requirements of your environment. For most Linux distributions, GVM is available through the package manager, making installation straightforward. Here's a general overview of the steps involved in setting up GVM:

1. Install GVM: Use your distribution's package manager to install GVM. For example, on Debian-based systems, you can use `sudo apt-get install gvm`.

2. Configure the Scanner: After installation, you may need to configure the scanner and other components. This could involve initializing the database and updating the vulnerability feed.

3. Start GVM Services: Ensure that all GVM components are running. This typically involves starting services like `gvmd`, `gsad`, and the scanner itself.

4. Access the GSA Web Interface: Open a web browser and navigate to the GSA web interface, usually hosted on port 9392 of the machine where GVM is installed.

Using GVM

Once GVM is installed and running, you can begin scanning your network for vulnerabilities:

1. Log in to GSA: Using the web interface, log in with your credentials.

2. Create a Target: Before scanning, you need to define a target. This is the IP address, range, or hostname of the system(s) you want to scan.

3. Configure and Run a Scan: Create a new scan task, selecting the target and the scan configuration. GVM comes with various scan configurations, ranging from fast and unobtrusive scans to deep, comprehensive scans.

4. Review Results: After the scan completes, review the results in the GSA interface. The results will include details about any vulnerabilities found, along with severity ratings and recommendations for remediation.

5. Manage and Remediate Vulnerabilities: Use the information provided by GVM to prioritize and address the vulnerabilities. GVM also allows for re-scanning and tracking the progress of your remediation efforts.

Best Practices for Using GVM
- Regularly Update the Vulnerability Feed: Ensure that your GVM installation regularly updates its vulnerability feed to include the latest vulnerability tests for accurate scanning.

- Schedule Regular Scans: Regular scanning helps in identifying new vulnerabilities as they emerge and in tracking the effectiveness of your remediation efforts.

- Carefully Plan Scans: To minimize the impact on network and system performance, plan your scans for off-peak hours. Consider the network load and the potential impact on critical systems.

- Review and Act on Results: Regularly review scan results, prioritize vulnerabilities based on their severity and potential impact, and take appropriate remediation actions.

GVM is a powerful tool for identifying and managing vulnerabilities, but like any tool, its effectiveness depends on how it's used. Regular, thoughtful vulnerability management practices are essential for maintaining a secure and resilient IT environment.

Nessus

Nessus is one of the most widely recognized vulnerability scanners in the **Cybersecurity** field, developed by Tenable Network Security. It is designed to automate the process of identifying and prioritizing vulnerabilities on various networked devices, such as servers, network devices, and operating systems, helping organizations to mitigate vulnerabilities before they can be exploited by attackers. Nessus is known for its robust detection capabilities, extensive plugin library, and ease of use. It can scan for vulnerabilities, misconfigurations, and even compliance with certain policies and standards.

Key Features of Nessus

- Comprehensive Vulnerability Coverage: Nessus scans for a wide range of vulnerabilities, including software flaws, missing patches, malware, and misconfigurations, across a variety of operating systems and applications.

- High-Speed Scanning: It efficiently scans large networks quickly, minimizing the impact on network performance.

- Regular Updates: Its plugin library is regularly updated to include the latest vulnerability checks, ensuring comprehensive coverage of new vulnerabilities.

- Customizable Reports: Nessus allows for detailed reporting, which can be customized to meet the needs of different stakeholders, from technical staff to executive management.

- Policy Compliance Checks: Beyond just identifying vulnerabilities, Nessus can also check systems for compliance with various security policies and standards.

Getting Started with Nessus
Nessus is available in several editions, including Nessus Professional for security practitioners and smaller organizations, and Nessus Manager for larger enterprise environments. Here's how to get started with Nessus Professional:

1. Download and Install Nessus: Visit the Tenable website to purchase or obtain a trial version of Nessus Professional. After downloading, install it on your chosen system following the provided instructions.

2. Activate Nessus: During the installation process, you will be prompted to enter an activation code, which you receive upon purchasing or registering for a trial.

3. Access the Nessus Web Interface: Once installed, Nessus can be accessed via a web browser. By default, the Nessus web interface runs on https://localhost:8834. You will need to create an account to start using it.

4. Configure and Run a Scan: From the web interface, you can configure new scans by specifying the target IP addresses or ranges and selecting the type of scan you want to run. Nessus provides several pre-configured templates to choose from, depending on your needs.

   - Create a New Scan: Click on "New Scan" and choose a template (e.g., Basic Network Scan, Web Application Tests, Advanced Scan).

- Configure Scan Settings: Enter the details of your scan, including targets, scan name, and any specific settings or credentials that Nessus needs to perform a thorough scan.

- Launch the Scan: After configuring your scan, launch it. The duration will depend on the number of targets and the scan configuration.

5. Review Scan Results: Once the scan is complete, Nessus will provide a detailed report of the findings, including the severity of each vulnerability found. The report can also suggest remediation steps for addressing identified vulnerabilities.

6. Act on the Findings: Prioritize vulnerabilities based on their severity and potential impact on your environment. Develop a remediation plan to address the vulnerabilities, starting with the most critical ones.

Best Practices for Using Nessus
- Regular Scanning: Regularly scan your environment to detect new vulnerabilities, especially after making changes to your network or applications.

- Scan Configuration: Tailor your scan configurations to match your environment and the specific areas you want to test. This can help reduce false positives and focus on the most relevant vulnerabilities.

- Access Management: Manage access to Nessus carefully, especially when configuring scans that use credentials to perform authenticated scans.

- Stay Informed: Keep abreast of the latest vulnerabilities and threats, and ensure your Nessus plugins are up to date, to maintain effective detection capabilities.

Nessus is a powerful tool for enhancing your Cybersecurity posture by identifying vulnerabilities before they can be exploited. By integrating Nessus into your regular security practices, you can significantly improve your organization's ability to defend against cyber threats.

Access Control List (ACL)

An Access Control List (ACL) is a set of rules that is used to filter network traffic and control network access based on specified criteria. Essentially, ACLs are a tool used by network devices (such as routers and switches) to permit or deny the forwarding of traffic entering or exiting a network interface based on a set of guidelines. These guidelines are determined by network administrators and can be based on several attributes including IP addresses, protocols (e.g., TCP, UDP), ports, or even time of day for more advanced configurations.

Types of ACLs
There are primarily two types of ACLs:

1. Standard ACLs: These are simpler and control traffic based solely on the source IP address. They are used to permit or deny the entire suite of protocols from a specific IP address or range of addresses.

2. Extended ACLs: These offer more granularity and can filter traffic based on both source and destination IP addresses, protocol types, ports, and other criteria. Extended ACLs allow for a more detailed and specific approach to traffic management, making them suitable for controlling access to specific services or applications.

How ACLs Work
-Permit and Deny Statements: ACLs work by processing "permit" and "deny" statements (or rules) that are defined by the administrator. These statements are checked sequentially until a match is found. If no match is found, the default action is typically to deny the traffic.

-Direction and Placement: ACLs can be applied to inbound or outbound traffic on network interfaces. The placement of ACLs is

crucial for their effectiveness. For instance, placing an ACL on the inbound traffic of an external interface can prevent unwanted access from external sources.

Uses of ACLs

-Security: ACLs are a fundamental security tool used to restrict unauthorized access to network resources by blocking potentially harmful traffic.

- Traffic Control- They can manage and limit the flow of traffic through a network, which can be crucial for network performance and bandwidth management.

- Network Segmentation: ACLs can be used to create segments within a network, restricting access between them as a method of isolating sensitive areas of a network or implementing a basic form of network segmentation.

- Policy Enforcement: ACLs enforce policies for network access, ensuring that only permitted traffic as defined by the organization's policies can access certain network segments or resources.

Considerations

- Maintenance: As network configurations change, ACLs require updating to ensure they remain effective and relevant.

-Performance Impact: Incorrectly configured or overly complex ACLs can negatively impact network performance.

-Security Limitations: While ACLs are a valuable tool for basic traffic filtering and access control, they should be part of a layered security approach due to their limitations in dealing with more sophisticated threats.

Access Control Lists are a crucial component of network management and security, providing a mechanism for enforcing access policies and controlling traffic flow across network boundaries. Their effectiveness, however, relies on careful planning, configuration, and maintenance by network administrators.

In one of my engagements, the organization prided itself on the robust security of its Access Control List (ACL) rules, particularly boasting about the impermeability of their guest network against unauthorized access to their backend systems. Upon receiving their ACL documentation— a daunting 60 pages printed double-sided— for review, it became evident before even attempting a connection that the vast majority of these rules were essentially nullified. Buried on the second page was an 'allow all' rule that went unnoticed, rendering the subsequent 58 pages of detailed restrictions ineffective. As anticipated, during my penetration testing, I effortlessly accessed all their servers via the guest network. This incident underscores the importance of diligent ACL management. ACLs are indeed powerful security mechanisms, but their efficacy is contingent on meticulous maintenance and regular review. Adding a rule should always be approached with caution, ensuring it aligns with the existing framework without inadvertently compromising the system's integrity.

Firewalls

Firewalls are critical security devices or software that monitor and control the incoming and outgoing network traffic based on an organization's previously defined security policies. At their core, firewalls serve to establish a barrier between your secure internal network and untrusted external networks, such as the internet, to prevent unauthorized access and potential threats. Let's break down the different types of firewalls and their specific roles, particularly focusing on network firewalls, application firewalls, and endpoint firewalls.

Types of Firewalls:

1. Network Firewalls

These are positioned at the gateway between your private network and the public internet or between different segments of your network. Network firewalls can be hardware-based, software-based, or a combination of both, and are designed to filter traffic based on IP addresses, domain names, and protocols. They can be further categorized into:

- Packet Filtering Firewalls: The simplest form, which inspects packets individually without considering the context of the overall connection.

- Stateful Inspection Firewalls: More advanced than packet filters, these track the state of active connections and make decisions based on the context of the traffic and sessions.

- Next-Generation Firewalls (NGFW): These combine the capabilities of traditional firewalls with advanced features like deep packet inspection, intrusion prevention systems, and application awareness.

Importance:
Network Firewalls:

- Protection at Network Perimeter: Serve as the first line of defense against external threats.

- Traffic Filtering: Control access to network resources based on IP addresses, domain names, and protocols.

- Segmentation: Help in segmenting different parts of a network for enhanced security.

2. Application Firewalls (Web Application Firewalls - WAF)
Focused on applications, these firewalls filter traffic to and from a specific application or set of applications. They work at the application layer to inspect the content of the traffic, looking for malicious requests and blocking attacks such as SQL injection, cross-site scripting (XSS), and other exploits that target vulnerabilities in web applications. WAFs can be implemented as appliance-based solutions, cloud services, or integrated into application code.

Importance:
Application Firewalls (WAF):

- Application-Specific Protection: Provide tailored security measures for specific applications, addressing their unique vulnerabilities.

- Prevent Application Attacks: Protect against application layer attacks, such as SQL injection, XSS, and others that traditional network firewalls might not catch.

3. Endpoint Firewalls
These are software-based firewalls installed on individual devices (endpoints) like laptops, desktops, and servers. Endpoint firewalls control the inbound and outbound connections initiated by the

device itself, offering a layer of protection at the device level. They can prevent malicious software from making external connections and can restrict lateral movement within a network if a device is compromised.

Importance:
Endpoint Firewalls:

- Device-Level Security: Offer a security layer at the individual device level, protecting against threats that bypass network defenses.

- Controlled Access: Manage application access to network resources and the internet, preventing potentially harmful communications.

Combining network firewalls, application firewalls, and endpoint firewalls provides a comprehensive defense mechanism across different layers of the network architecture. This multi-layered approach ensures that an organization's critical assets are protected from various angles, significantly reducing the risk of cyber threats and data breaches

---

One notable example of a breach caused by firewall misconfiguration is the Capital One data breach that occurred in March 2019. In this incident, a former Amazon Web Services (AWS) engineer exploited a misconfigured web application firewall (WAF) to access the data of over 100 million Capital One customers. The vulnerability allowed the attacker to gain access to Capital One's AWS environment, where they were able to obtain sensitive data, including names, addresses, credit scores, and social security numbers.
The misconfiguration involved an improperly set up WAF, which is intended to filter and monitor incoming traffic to a web application for malicious attempts. However, in this case, the misconfiguration allowed the attacker to execute a series of commands that exploited the WAF's vulnerability, ultimately granting unauthorized access to the data stored on Capital One's AWS servers.

This breach underscores the importance of proper security configuration and regular security audits to identify and rectify potential vulnerabilities. It also highlights the complex nature of cloud environments, where the responsibility for security is shared between the cloud service provider and the client. In the aftermath, Capital One was fined $80 million by regulatory authorities for its failure to establish effective risk management practices and for not fixing the known vulnerability in a timely manner.

VLANs (Virtual Local Area Networks)

A VLAN is a subgroup within a network, which partitions and isolates network devices into separate, distinct segments at the data link layer (Layer 2) of the OSI (Open Systems Interconnection) model. This segmentation is purely logical and does not depend on the physical location of the devices, allowing for more flexible and efficient network management.

Key Benefits and Features of VLANs:

Improved Security: By segmenting a network into VLANs, network administrators can apply security policies to specific groups of users or devices, reducing the risk of internal threats and data breaches.

Reduced Congestion: VLANs limit broadcast traffic to devices within the same VLAN, which can significantly reduce unnecessary network traffic and enhance performance.

Enhanced Flexibility: Devices can be grouped by function or department rather than their physical location, simplifying network management and supporting more efficient resource allocation.

Simpler Policy Enforcement: Network policies, such as quality of service (QoS) and access controls, can be more easily applied and managed within VLANs.

Virtual Routers

A virtual router is a software-based routing framework that replicates the functionality of a physical router. It runs on general hardware within a virtual environment (as a virtual machine) or as part of a larger software system. Virtual routers use software applications to route information and perform other functions of a hardware-based router, including traffic directing and network protocols management.

Key Benefits and Features of Virtual Routers:
Cost-Effectiveness: Virtual routers can reduce the need for physical routers, saving on hardware costs and the expenses associated with hardware maintenance and power consumption.

Flexibility and Scalability: It's easier to deploy, manage, and scale virtual routers as network demands change, without the need for additional physical space or hardware.

Redundancy and Reliability: Deploying multiple virtual routers can enhance network reliability and redundancy, ensuring continuous network service even if one virtual instance fails.

Rapid Deployment: Virtual routers can be quickly configured and deployed to meet immediate networking needs, supporting dynamic network environments and testing scenarios.

Virtual routers are part of a broader move towards more flexible, software-defined networking solutions. By decoupling the network's logical structure from its physical infrastructure, these technologies allow for more agile, efficient, and cost-effective network management, supporting the diverse and evolving needs of modern organizations and network environments.

Endpoint Detection and Response (EDR)

Endpoint Detection and Response (EDR) is a **Cybersecurity** solution focused on detecting, investigating, and mitigating suspicious activities and issues on hosts and endpoints. Essentially, EDR systems are tools designed to help security teams quickly identify and respond to threats at the endpoint level, where traditional security measures may fail to detect advanced attacks. The emergence of EDR solutions marks a significant evolution in endpoint security, moving beyond simple prevention to include detection, investigation, and response capabilities.

Key Features of EDR
EDR solutions are characterized by several key features:

- Continuous Monitoring and Data Collection: EDR systems continuously monitor and gather data from endpoints to identify potential security threats. This data can include system processes, network communication, and file activities.

- Threat Detection: Utilizing advanced analytics, machine learning, and behavior analysis, EDR tools can detect anomalies, patterns, and behaviors indicative of potential threats, including malware, ransomware, and sophisticated persistent attacks.

- Alerts and Notifications: When a potential threat is detected, EDR systems generate alerts to notify security personnel, providing detailed information about the suspicious activity.

- Investigation and Forensics: EDR solutions offer tools for investigating and understanding the scope and impact of a threat. This includes tracing the origin of an attack, identifying affected systems, and determining the data or credentials that may have been compromised.

- Response and Mitigation: Beyond detection, EDR tools provide mechanisms for responding to and mitigating threats. This can range from isolating infected endpoints from the network to automatically removing or containing malicious files.

- Integration with Other Security Tools: Many EDR solutions can integrate with other security systems, such as Security Information and Event Management (SIEM) systems, firewalls, and threat intelligence platforms, to enhance overall security posture.

Importance of EDR
The importance of EDR in modern **Cybersecurity** strategies is underscored by several factors:

- Evolving Threat Landscape: As cyber threats become more sophisticated, traditional antivirus and anti-malware solutions are often insufficient. EDR provides enhanced capabilities to detect and respond to advanced threats.

- Insider Threats and Lateral Movement: EDR can help identify suspicious behaviors and activities that may indicate insider threats or attempts by attackers to move laterally within a network.

- Compliance and Regulatory Requirements: Many industries have regulations that require companies to have measures in place for detecting and responding to **Cybersecurity** incidents. EDR can help fulfill these requirements.

- Detailed Incident Analysis and Response: EDR provides detailed forensic capabilities, enabling organizations to thoroughly investigate incidents, understand the impact, and respond effectively to mitigate damage.

Application Control

Application control is a critical security practice that involves restricting unauthorized applications from executing in an organization's network. This **Cybersecurity** measure helps in managing and controlling the software that can run on a system, thereby minimizing the attack surface and reducing the risk of malware infections and other security threats. Application control policies are enforced through various means, including whitelisting, blacklisting, and graylisting of applications, providing a robust framework for securing IT environments against unauthorized and potentially harmful software.

Importance of Application Control

The significance of application control in **Cybersecurity** cannot be overstated, as it addresses several key security challenges and objectives:

1. Mitigating Malware Risks: By allowing only approved applications to run, application control significantly reduces the risk of malware infections. Malicious programs and scripts are prevented from executing, thereby stopping many attacks in their tracks.

2. Preventing Zero-day Attacks: Zero-day vulnerabilities are unknown flaws in software that can be exploited by attackers before the vendor releases a patch. Application control can mitigate the risk of zero-day attacks by restricting the execution of unauthorized software that might exploit such vulnerabilities.

3. Reducing Attack Surface: Application control policies help in minimizing the attack surface by ensuring that only necessary applications are running on the system. This reduces the number of potential targets for attackers and simplifies security management.

4. Enforcing Software Compliance: In many regulated industries, organizations are required to ensure that only licensed and approved software is used. Application control helps in enforcing compliance with these requirements, avoiding legal and financial penalties.

5. Improving System Performance: By controlling the applications that can run on a system, organizations can prevent unauthorized or unnecessary software from consuming system resources. This can lead to improved system performance and reliability.

6. Protecting Sensitive Information: Application control can prevent data exfiltration by blocking unauthorized applications that might attempt to transmit sensitive information outside the organization.

Implementing Application Control
Effective application control involves several steps, including:

- Inventorying Authorized Applications: Organizations must first identify and catalog all authorized software that is necessary for business operations. This list serves as the basis for whitelisting applications.

- Establishing Policies: Define clear policies for managing and controlling applications, including criteria for whitelisting, procedures for updating the whitelist, and actions to take against unauthorized applications.

- Deploying Application Control Solutions: Implement application control tools or features within endpoint protection platforms to enforce policies. These solutions can range from basic whitelisting features to advanced application control frameworks with detailed rules and exceptions.

- Monitoring and Auditing: Regularly monitor application control logs and audit the effectiveness of the control measures. This helps in identifying potential security issues and adjusting policies as needed.

- User Education and Communication: Educate users about the application control policies and the importance of using only authorized software. Clear communication helps in ensuring compliance and minimizing disruptions to business operations.

Encryption

Encryption is a process that transforms readable data, known as plaintext, into a coded form called ciphertext, making it unreadable to unauthorized users. This transformation is achieved using algorithms and encryption keys. The primary purpose of encryption is to protect the confidentiality of digital data stored on computer systems or transmitted via the internet or other computer networks. Decryption is the reverse process, turning the ciphertext back into plaintext, accessible only to those who possess the correct decryption key or password.

Importance of Encryption

The importance of encryption spans various aspects of digital security and privacy, making it indispensable in today's digital world:

1. Data Protection: Encryption ensures that sensitive data, such as personal information, financial details, and confidential documents, is kept secure from unauthorized access, whether it's stored on devices or in transit over networks.

2. Privacy Assurance: With the increasing concerns over personal privacy, encryption helps individuals maintain their privacy by protecting personal messages, emails, and other forms of communication from being intercepted and read by third parties.

3. Security in E-commerce: Encryption is fundamental to the security of online transactions. It protects credit card information and personal data from being stolen by cybercriminals during online purchases, fostering trust in e-commerce systems.

4. Regulatory Compliance: Many industries are governed by regulations that require the protection of sensitive data.

Encryption helps organizations comply with these regulations, such as GDPR, HIPAA, and PCI-DSS, which mandate strict measures for data security.

5. Protection Against Cyber Threats: Encryption mitigates the risks associated with various cyber threats, including data breaches, hacking, and identity theft. Even if data is intercepted or a system is breached, encrypted data remains unreadable and useless to attackers without the decryption key.

6. Secure Communication: Encryption is essential for secure communication over the internet, including emails, messaging apps, and voice or video calls, ensuring that only the intended recipients can access the content of the communication.

7. Data Integrity: Some forms of encryption also provide data integrity, ensuring that the data has not been tampered with or altered during storage or transmission.

Types of Encryption
There are two primary types of encryption:

Symmetric Encryption: Uses the same key for both encryption and decryption. It's faster and more efficient, making it suitable for encrypting large volumes of data. However, key distribution and management can be challenging, as the key must be securely shared between parties.

Asymmetric Encryption: Uses a pair of keys, a public key for encryption and a private key for decryption. This type overcomes the key distribution problem of symmetric encryption, as the public key can be shared openly, while the private key is kept secret. It's commonly used for secure communications, digital signatures, and key exchange.

In the early 2000s, during the beginning stages of social media, security measures on these platforms were not as robust as they are today. It was a period when social media was gaining popularity but the awareness of security protocols, such as encrypted network traffic, were still evolving. During this time, it was not unheard of for individuals, such as students at universities, to engage in network sniffing—a method where one monitors and analyzes network traffic for data such as usernames and passwords. This network sniffing could be done via wired or wireless capture.

Social media sites initially did not encrypt their network traffic, which meant that when users logged in, their credentials were transmitted over the network in plain text. This lack of encryption made it relatively easy for someone with the right tools and a malicious intent to capture these credentials and gain unauthorized access to others' social media accounts. The practice exposed a significant vulnerability in the early design of social media platforms.

As the digital landscape matured and the need for enhanced security became evident, social media platforms began implementing encryption protocols, such as HTTPS, to secure the data transmission between the user's device and the social media servers. This shift marked a significant step in protecting users' privacy and security, making it much more difficult for unauthorized individuals to intercept and decipher sensitive information.

Patch Management

Patch management is a critical process within the realm of **Cybersecurity** and IT management, focusing on the regular acquisition, testing, and installation of patches (updates or fixes) to software and systems. These patches can address security vulnerabilities, fix bugs, or add new features. Efficient patch management is essential for maintaining the operational integrity and security of IT systems.

Importance of Patch Management

The importance of patch management stems from its role in safeguarding digital assets from evolving cyber threats, ensuring system reliability, and maintaining regulatory compliance:

1. Security Vulnerability Mitigation: One of the primary reasons for applying patches is to correct security vulnerabilities in software and operating systems. Hackers and cybercriminals exploit these vulnerabilities to launch attacks. Regular patching closes these security gaps, significantly reducing the risk of breaches and attacks.

2. Preventing Exploits: Many cyber-attacks use known vulnerabilities that have already been patched by vendors. Effective patch management ensures that these vulnerabilities are promptly addressed, preventing exploitation by malware, ransomware, and other cyber threats.

3. Compliance with Regulations: Various industry regulations and standards (such as GDPR, HIPAA, and PCI DSS) require businesses to protect data by maintaining up-to-date systems. Regular patching is a key requirement for compliance, helping avoid potential fines and legal issues.

4. System Stability and Performance: Patches not only address security issues but also fix bugs that can cause system crashes, errors, or performance degradation. By keeping systems updated, organizations can ensure more stable and efficient operations.

5. Enhancing Features and Functionality: Some patches include enhancements and new features that can improve the functionality and efficiency of software and systems, providing businesses with new tools and capabilities.

Challenges in Patch Management
Despite its importance, patch management presents several challenges:

- Volume and Complexity: With the vast number of applications and systems in use within an organization, managing and prioritizing patches can be complex.

- Risk of Disruption: Applying patches can sometimes introduce new issues or incompatibilities, potentially disrupting business operations.

- Resource Intensive: The process requires time and resources to test and deploy patches across multiple systems and environments.

Best Practices for Patch Management
To address these challenges and ensure an effective patch management strategy, organizations should consider the following best practices:

- Automate Patch Management: Use automated tools to streamline the patch management process, including the detection of needed updates, prioritization, and deployment.

- Prioritize Based on Risk: Assess the criticality of vulnerabilities and prioritize patches based on the potential impact on the organization.

- Test Before Deployment: Test patches in a controlled environment to ensure they do not introduce new issues before widespread deployment.

- Maintain an Inventory: Keep an up-to-date inventory of all systems and software in use, to ensure no assets are overlooked during the patching process.

- Educate and Train Staff: Ensure IT staff are aware of the importance of patch management and are trained in best practices.

Patch management is an essential component of a proactive **Cybersecurity** posture, helping organizations protect against vulnerabilities, comply with regulations, and ensure the smooth operation of IT systems. Despite its challenges, adopting best practices and leveraging automation can make patch management a manageable and integral part of an organization's IT strategy.

Password Management

Password management is a critical aspect of **Cybersecurity**, involving the creation, storage, and maintenance of passwords in a secure and efficient manner. It plays a pivotal role in protecting an organization's digital assets by ensuring that access to systems, applications, and data is securely controlled. Effective password management helps in preventing unauthorized access, thereby reducing the risk of data breaches and cyber-attacks.

Importance of Password Management

- Stronger Security: Password management encourages the use of strong, unique passwords for each account or system, significantly reducing the risk of brute force attacks and unauthorized access.

- Reducing Password Reuse: By managing passwords securely, individuals are less likely to reuse passwords across multiple sites and systems, a common practice that can lead to multiple accounts being compromised if one password is exposed.

- Enhancing User Convenience: With secure password management solutions, such as password managers, users can maintain complex and unique passwords without the need to remember them all, improving both security and user experience.

- Efficient Recovery: Good password management includes mechanisms for securely recovering or resetting lost or forgotten passwords, ensuring that users can regain access to their accounts without compromising security.

- Compliance: Many regulatory standards require secure password management practices to protect sensitive information, making effective password management essential for compliance.

Integrating Physical Management of Passwords

In addition to digital strategies, the physical management of passwords demands equal attention. It is imperative to educate users on the dangers of writing down passwords and storing them in unsecured locations, such as under keyboards or attached to badges. Such practices can inadvertently lead to unauthorized access, especially in shared or public spaces. Encouraging a culture of security awareness where physical and digital password management practices are respected is key to fortifying an organization's defense against threats.

Layers of **Cybersecurity** and Password Management

Password management is an integral part of Identity and Access Management (IAM), which is one of the foundational layers of **Cybersecurity**. IAM encompasses the policies and technologies that ensure the right individuals have access to the appropriate resources at the right times for the right reasons. Passwords are a fundamental component of the authentication process, where a user's identity is verified before access is granted to systems or data.

Password management intersects with other layers of **Cybersecurity** as well, reinforcing the importance of a holistic security approach:

- Endpoint Security: Secure password practices protect endpoints (e.g., laptops, smartphones) by preventing unauthorized access, even if the device is lost or stolen.

- Data Security: By safeguarding access to systems and applications, effective password management plays a direct role in protecting the data stored within these resources.

- Application Security: Secure authentication mechanisms, including password management, are crucial for protecting applications from unauthorized access and potential exploitation.

Effective password management is crucial for maintaining the security and integrity of an organization's digital assets. As a key component of Identity and Access Management, it plays a vital role in securing access to systems, data, and applications, thereby protecting against unauthorized use and cyber threats. By implementing strong password policies and encouraging the use of password management tools, organizations can significantly enhance their overall **Cybersecurity** posture.

In the realm of password management, some of the most straightforward breaches I've encountered in organizations were a result of passwords carelessly left under keyboards or attached to badges. Such placements often make them susceptible to being inadvertently revealed during casual encounters, such as when someone exits as another person enters a room. Therefore, it's imperative to emphasize not only the importance of diligent password management but also the necessity of regularly verifying adherence to these practices. Education on secure password handling, coupled with consistent enforcement of security policies, is crucial in fortifying an organization's defenses against unauthorized access.

Phishing

The methodology used to create and execute a phishing attack involves several stages, from planning and target selection to the actual deployment of the phishing messages and the collection of stolen data. Here's a general overview of the steps involved in a typical phishing attack:

1. Objective Setting
- Attackers define their goals, such as stealing login credentials, financial information, or installing malware on the victim's device.

2. Target Selection
- Attackers decide on their target audience, which can range from individuals to employees within a specific company or users of a particular service. They may conduct research to gather email addresses or other contact information.

3. Crafting the Message
- The phishing message is designed to look as legitimate as possible to trick the recipient into taking the desired action. This often involves mimicking the visual design, language, and tone of communications from a trusted entity, such as a bank, tech company, or governmental organization.

- The message typically includes a sense of urgency or a compelling reason for the recipient to respond, such as a security alert, a prize, or an account issue.

4. Creating the Payload
- Depending on the attack's objective, the payload may be a malicious link leading to a fake website where victims are prompted to enter personal information or download a file that contains malware.

- The fake website is often a close replica of a legitimate site, designed to deceive victims into believing they are interacting with the real entity.

5. Launching the Attack
- Attackers distribute the phishing messages through various channels, including email, SMS, social media, or instant messaging platforms. The distribution method is chosen based on the target audience and the likelihood of the message being opened and acted upon.

6. Collecting the Data
- If the attack involves a fake website, attackers collect the data entered by victims on the site. In cases where malware is used, the malicious software may gather information directly from the victim's device and send it back to the attacker.

7. Exploiting the Stolen Information
- The attackers use the stolen information for their original objective, which may involve accessing bank accounts, selling personal information, or leveraging stolen credentials for further attacks.

8. Covering Tracks
- Sophisticated attackers may take steps to hide their activities and maintain access to compromised systems without being detected.

Countermeasures and Prevention
Organizations and individuals can adopt various strategies to protect against phishing attacks, including:

- Education and training to recognize phishing attempts

- Using spam filters and security software to detect and block phishing messages

- Implementing multi-factor authentication (MFA) to reduce the impact of compromised credentials

- Regularly updating and patching software to protect against malware

Understanding the methodology behind phishing attacks is crucial for developing effective countermeasures and reducing the risk of falling victim to these increasingly sophisticated and damaging cyber threats.

The 2017 NotPetya cyberattack provides a stark example of how devastating poor patch management can be, affecting businesses and governments worldwide. NotPetya was initially spread through a compromised Ukrainian software called M.E.Doc, used for tax accounting. It exploited vulnerabilities in Microsoft Windows, particularly one known as EternalBlue, for which Microsoft had released a patch several months before the attack began. Despite the availability of this patch, many organizations had not applied it, leaving their systems vulnerable. NotPetya was particularly damaging because it masqueraded as ransomware but was designed primarily to destroy data. It caused billions of dollars in damage across multiple countries, affecting major corporations, including shipping giant Maersk, multinational pharmaceutical company Merck, and FedEx's European subsidiary TNT Express, among others.

*The incident underscores the importance of timely patch management and the potential for significant financial and operational impacts when patches for known vulnerabilities are not applied promptly. The widespread damage caused by NotPetya highlighted the global interconnectedness of businesses and the need for robust **Cybersecurity** practices to protect against sophisticated cyber threats.*

Multi-factor authentication (MFA)

Multi-factor authentication (MFA) is a security mechanism that requires individuals to verify their identity by providing two or more verification factors before they can access a resource, such as an application, online account, or a VPN. Instead of merely asking for a username and password, MFA requires one or more additional verification factors, which significantly increases the security of user logins and protects against various forms of cyber threats, including phishing, social engineering, and brute force attacks.

Components of MFA

MFA verification factors are generally categorized into three main types:

1. Something You Know: This includes knowledge-based factors like passwords, PINs, or answers to security questions.

2. Something You Have: This involves possession-based factors such as a security token, a smartphone app (like an authenticator app that generates time-based one-time passwords, or TOTP), a smart card, or a hardware token.

3. Something You Are: This category includes biometric factors, such as fingerprint scans, facial recognition, voice recognition, or iris scans.

How MFA Works

When MFA is enabled, the system will prompt the user for their usual login credentials — for example, a username and password (something you know). Then, instead of immediately granting access, the system will require an additional verification step, such as entering a code received on the user's smartphone (something you have) or scanning a fingerprint (something you are).

Advantages of MFA

Enhanced Security: By requiring multiple forms of verification, MFA makes it significantly more difficult for unauthorized users to access a target, even if they have compromised one of the authentication factors (like the password).

Compliance: Many regulations and standards, such as GDPR, HIPAA, and PCI-DSS, recommend or require MFA to protect sensitive data.

Flexibility and Scalability: Organizations can implement various MFA methods to suit their security needs and user preferences, offering flexibility in how authentication is managed.

Considerations

While MFA significantly enhances security, it's important to choose the right combination of factors for your organization, balancing security needs with user convenience. Overly complex MFA implementations can lead to user frustration and reduced productivity, so it's crucial to implement MFA in a user-friendly manner. Additionally, organizations should educate their users on the importance of MFA and provide clear instructions on how to use it effectively.

Network Access Control (NAC)

Network Access Control (NAC) is a security solution that manages and restricts the access of devices to a network based on defined security policies. At its core, NAC helps ensure that only authorized and compliant devices can access network resources, thus protecting the network from potential threats introduced by non-compliant or infected devices. Here's a breakdown of how NAC works and its key components:

How NAC Works

1. Authentication: When a device attempts to connect to the network, NAC solutions first authenticate the user or the device, verifying their identity through credentials, digital certificates, or other authentication methods.

2. Posture Assessment: After authentication, NAC evaluates the security posture of the device. This involves checking if the device complies with the organization's security policies, such as having the latest antivirus updates, required software patches, and correct configurations.

3. Access Control: Based on the authentication and posture assessment, NAC then enforces access control policies. Devices that meet the security requirements are allowed access to the network, possibly with restrictions based on their compliance level, role, location, or other attributes. Non-compliant devices may be denied access, placed in a quarantine network where they can be remediated, or given limited access to a subset of resources.

4. Continuous Monitoring and Response: NAC solutions continuously monitor connected devices for changes in compliance status. If a device becomes non-compliant while connected (e.g., due to a malware infection or disabling the firewall), NAC can automatically reevaluate and adjust the device's network access accordingly.

Key Benefits of NAC
- Enhanced Security: By ensuring that only compliant devices can access the network, NAC significantly reduces the risk of malware infections and data breaches.

- Compliance Management: NAC helps organizations comply with regulatory standards by enforcing security policies across all devices accessing the network.

- Visibility and Control: Provides comprehensive visibility into every device on the network, including BYOD (Bring Your Own Device) and IoT (Internet of Things) devices, allowing for better control and management of network access.

- Automated Incident Response: Automates responses to security incidents by restricting access for compromised devices, thereby containing threats and minimizing their impact.

Implementation Considerations
Implementing NAC can be complex, involving careful planning and customization to align with an organization's specific security policies and network architecture. Factors to consider include the types of devices accessing the network, the level of security required, the existing network infrastructure, and the need for integration with other security solutions.

NAC has evolved to address the challenges of modern networks, such as increased mobility, the proliferation of wireless access, and the diversity of devices connecting to networks. As part of a comprehensive security strategy, NAC plays a critical role in protecting network resources against unauthorized access and cyber threats.

No two Network Access Control (NAC) systems are identical, underscoring the importance of staying vigilant about any potential vulnerabilities they might introduce. In the early stages of NAC technology, many providers featured the capability for MAC (Media Access Control) filtering, leveraging the unique Layer 2 address inherent to network devices. This address, where the initial three octets identify the device's manufacturer, facilitated the association of devices with specific users within the network. The appeal of this software was magnified by its ability to not only register devices but also to catalog the operating systems, attributing each to a particular individual. However, this perceived security marvel was not infallible. An intriguing incident surfaced when, upon scrutinizing the logs, I encountered a MAC address affiliated with Sony, tagged to a Linux system—a configuration alien to our network's ecosystem. The source was traced back to an office where an individual had ingeniously altered their Linux machine to mimic their PlayStation's MAC address. This act of spoofing allowed them to bypass the system's controls, registering and incorporating an unauthorized device into the network. This incident serves as a poignant reminder of the ingenuity of workaround strategies and the continuous need for rigorous oversight in NAC implementations.

(IPS) & (IDS)

Intrusion Prevention Systems (IPS) and Intrusion Detection Systems (IDS) are critical components in the **Cybersecurity** defenses of an organization, playing crucial roles in identifying and managing potential threats. Both are designed to monitor network and system activities for malicious activities or policy violations, but they differ primarily in how they respond to these detections.

Intrusion Detection Systems (IDS)

Functionality: An IDS monitors network and system traffic for suspicious activities and potential violations of defined policies. It's essentially a detection tool that alerts system administrators or security personnel when it detects potentially malicious activity.

Types of IDS:

1. Network Intrusion Detection Systems (NIDS): Monitors the entire network for suspicious traffic by analyzing the traffic passing through the network.

2. Host Intrusion Detection Systems (HIDS): Installed on individual hosts (servers, workstations) to monitor inbound and outbound packets from the device only, and alerting on suspicious activity.

Response: When an IDS detects a potential threat, it logs the information and alerts administrators but does not take action to block or prevent the intrusion. It's up to the security team to analyze the alerts and take appropriate action.

Intrusion Prevention Systems (IPS)

Functionality: An IPS, often considered an extension of an IDS, not only detects suspicious activities but also takes proactive steps to prevent the threat from carrying out its intended action.

Types of IPS:

1. Network-based IPS (NIPS): Monitors the entire network for malicious activities by analyzing network traffic flows. It can prevent attacks from spreading by automatically taking action to block malicious traffic.

2. Host-based IPS (HIPS): Similar to HIDS, but with the ability to take direct action on the host to block malicious activities.

Response: IPS systems are designed to not only alert administrators of suspicious activities but also to automatically take predefined actions to prevent or mitigate the detected threat. These actions could include blocking traffic from a suspect IP address, closing maliciously opened network ports, or terminating malicious processes.

Key Differences
- Detection and Response: The primary difference between IDS and IPS lies in their response capabilities. While an IDS functions as an alert system for potential threats, an IPS takes direct action to block or prevent those threats based on its configurations.

- Deployment Position: IDS systems are typically deployed to monitor traffic, whereas IPS systems are strategically placed at points in the network where they can effectively prevent unauthorized access or malicious traffic from entering an environment.

Both IDS and IPS play vital roles in a comprehensive network security strategy, providing layers of defense that help protect an organization from cyber threats. The choice between deploying an IDS or IPS, or both, depends on the specific security requirements, the sensitivity of the data being protected, and the organization's policy towards managing potential threats

This tool has proven to be indispensable in the realm of network security. In the initial onslaught of the WannaCry outbreak, it seemed as though every organization within my sector was succumbing to infection. However, the Intrusion Prevention System (IPS) I utilized quickly adapted, releasing new definitions that enabled us to preemptively block any incoming traffic exhibiting the distinctive signature of the WannaCry virus. Although we also took the necessary steps to patch our systems, it was the IPS that made a remarkable difference, successfully thwarting over seven thousand intrusion attempts. This experience underscored the critical role of IPS in fortifying our network against such unprecedented cyber threats.

Group Policy

Group Policy is a feature in Windows that provides centralized management and configuration of operating systems, applications, and users' settings in an Active Directory environment. It allows network administrators to implement specific configurations for users and computers across the network. Through Group Policy, administrators can specify settings for numerous aspects of a user's desktop environment, which can include settings for network and Internet connections, desktop interfaces, security settings, and many others. Here are the basics:

Components of Group Policy

1. Group Policy Objects (GPOs): These are the key elements of Group Policy. They contain the settings made by administrators. Once created, they can be linked to an Active Directory site, domain, or organizational unit (OU).

2. Group Policy Management Console (GPMC): This is the tool provided by Microsoft to manage Group Policy. It's used to create, delete, link, and manage GPOs, as well as set security filtering and WMI filtering.

3. Client-Side Extensions (CSEs): These are components on the client computer that apply the settings configured in GPOs. Different CSEs correspond to different policy areas, such as software installation, scripts, folder redirection, and security settings.

4. Active Directory (AD): Group Policy relies heavily on AD for the application of policies to specific parts of the organization. AD's structure, including sites, domains, and OUs, determines how GPOs are applied.

How Group Policy Works

When a user logs in or a computer starts up, Group Policy is applied according to the location of the user or computer in the Active Directory hierarchy and any filters that are in place. GPOs can be enforced (making it difficult or impossible for users to override settings) or set to a lower priority, allowing some user customization. Policies are refreshed periodically in the background, ensuring that any changes to GPOs are applied consistently.

Finding Pre-Configured Security Policies

Microsoft provides several pre-configured security templates and tools to help administrators implement recommended security settings:

- Security Compliance Toolkit (SCT): This toolkit from Microsoft provides security baselines and best practices for a variety of Windows versions and other Microsoft software. It's an excellent starting point for securing your environment according to Microsoft's recommendations.

- Microsoft Security Baselines: Published as part of the Security Compliance Toolkit, these baselines are sets of recommended security settings that cover the various aspects of the Windows operating system, Microsoft Edge, and other Microsoft products. They are designed to provide a secure foundation that organizations can build upon.

You can find these resources on Microsoft's official website or by searching for the "Microsoft Security Compliance Toolkit" or "Microsoft Security Baselines." Additionally, the Center for Internet Security (CIS) offers another set of security benchmarks for Windows and other systems, which are widely respected in the industry. These can be found on the CIS website, though access to the full benchmarks might require membership.

It's important to review these policies and customize them according to the specific needs and security requirements of your organization.

Applying security settings without proper understanding can lead to unintended consequences, including impaired system functionality or usability.

USB Lock Down

Locking down external media, including USB ports, is a security measure taken to prevent unauthorized access, data leakage, or the introduction of malware into a system. This can be particularly important in environments that handle sensitive information or where system integrity is critical. This is very common practice across the board and in most cases I have seen it where a group is made either in active directory or within the third party software to allow users to use USB when needed. Here's how you can lock down USB ports on a Windows machine:

1. Using Group Policy Editor to Lock Down USB
For Windows Professional or Enterprise editions, the Group Policy Editor is a powerful tool for system administrators to control the working environment of user accounts and computer accounts. Follow these steps to disable USB ports:

1. Press `Win + R`, type `gpedit.msc`, and press Enter to open the Group Policy Editor.

2. Navigate to `Computer Configuration` > `Administrative Templates` > `System` > `Removable Storage Access`.

3. In the right pane, find and double-click on `All Removable Storage classes: Deny all access`.

4. Select `Enabled` to deny access to all removable storage classes.

5. Click `Apply` and then `OK`.

2. Using Registry Editor to Lock Down USB

If you're using a version of Windows that doesn't include the Group Policy Editor, such as Home Editions, you can edit the Registry directly:

1. Press `Win + R`, type `regedit`, and press Enter to open the Registry Editor.

2. Navigate to `HKEY_LOCAL_MACHINE\SYSTEM\CurrentControlSet\Services\USBSTOR`.

3. In the right pane, double-click on `Start`.

4. Change the value to `4` (to disable USB storage) and click `OK`. The default value is `3` (USB storage enabled).

5. Close the Registry Editor and restart your computer for the changes to take effect.

3. Using Third-Party Software to Lock Down USB

There are also third-party applications available that can help manage USB port security. These tools can provide a more user-friendly interface for controlling access to USB ports and other external media. Some popular options include USB Lock, Ratool (Removable Access Tool), and USBDeview.

Important Considerations

- Backup: Before making system changes, especially in the Registry, it's wise to create a system restore point or back up the Registry. This way, you can revert the system back to its original state if something goes wrong.

- Security Policy Compliance: If you're implementing these changes in a corporate environment, ensure they comply with your organization's IT security policies.

- Regular Review: Security is not a one-time task. Regularly review your security measures to ensure they are still effective and update them as needed.

Locking down USB ports can significantly improve system security, but it's also essential to consider the operational impact, especially in environments where external media are frequently used for legitimate purposes.

One of the most notable incidents involving a security breach due to a USB drive occurred in 2008 with the U.S. Department of Defense (DoD). This incident, often referred to as the "worst breach of U.S. military computers in history," was initiated by a foreign intelligence agency using a USB drive.
The Incident:
The breach, known as "Operation Buckshot Yankee," began when a USB flash drive infected with malicious code was inserted into a laptop of the U.S. military located in the Middle East. The malware on the USB drive was designed to exploit vulnerabilities in Windows operating systems, and it spread rapidly across classified and unclassified military networks.
How the Malware Worked:
The malware, a variant of the SillyFDC worm, used autorun features to propagate itself across the network. It established a digital beachhead for the attackers, allowing them to relay back sensitive data to a foreign intelligence agency's server. The sophistication of the attack indicated that it was not the work of amateurs but a well-organized, state-sponsored entity.
Response and Aftermath:
The discovery of this breach led to a significant response from the DoD:
- The DoD banned the use of USB drives and other forms of removable media by its personnel, a ban that was temporarily enforced until new policies and technologies were put in place to secure the use of such devices.
- It accelerated the DoD's efforts to develop and implement more robust cybersecurity measures, including the use of encrypted USB drives, stricter access controls, and enhanced monitoring of network and system activities.
- The incident underscored the need for continuous vigilance, the importance of securing endpoints, and the potential vulnerabilities introduced by seemingly innocuous devices like USB drives.

Lessons Learned:
The Operation Buckshot Yankee incident highlighted several critical cybersecurity lessons:
- Endpoint Security: The importance of securing all endpoints, not just network perimeters, as attackers can exploit any vulnerability to gain access.
- Insider Threat: The need to consider the insider threat, whether malicious or accidental, as significant as external threats.
- Policy and Training: The critical role of policy, training, and awareness in preventing security breaches. Users must understand the risks associated with removable media and other potential security threats.
- Rapid Response: The value of a rapid and coordinated response to contain and mitigate the effects of a breach.
This incident remains a pivotal case study in cybersecurity, illustrating the potential risks posed by removable media and the importance of comprehensive security strategies to protect sensitive information and infrastructure.

Common Vulnerabilities and Exposures(CVE)

A CVE, or Common Vulnerabilities and Exposures, is a list of publicly disclosed cybersecurity vulnerabilities and exposures. Each entry, or CVE Record, in the list includes an identification number, a description, and at least one public reference for publicly known cybersecurity vulnerabilities. The main purpose of CVEs is to make it easier to share data across separate vulnerability capabilities (tools, databases, and services) with the cybersecurity community.

MITRE is a not-for-profit organization that manages the CVE Program. MITRE plays a crucial role in the cybersecurity ecosystem by providing a standardized identifier for a given vulnerability or exposure. This enables effective discussion, management, and mitigation of vulnerabilities by providing a common language for different stakeholders, including cybersecurity professionals, organizations, and software vendors. The importance of MITRE in managing CVEs includes:

1. Standardization: MITRE's management of the CVE list helps ensure that each vulnerability is described in a standardized way, making it easier for everyone in the cybersecurity field to understand and address vulnerabilities.

2. Coordination: MITRE coordinates with various vulnerability researchers, vendors, and databases, ensuring that information about vulnerabilities is collected, organized, and disseminated effectively.

3. Public Resource: The CVE list is freely available to the public, making it a valuable resource for researchers, IT professionals, and security experts for identifying and mitigating vulnerabilities in software and hardware.

4. Enhanced Security: By providing a comprehensive and up-to-date list of vulnerabilities, MITRE helps organizations improve their security posture by enabling them to quickly identify and address potential threats to their systems.

5. Community Engagement: MITRE engages with the global cybersecurity community, facilitating collaboration and the sharing of expertise and information. This community-driven approach helps in the rapid identification and resolution of vulnerabilities.

Overall, MITRE's management of the CVE Program is vital for ensuring that vulnerabilities are properly identified, cataloged, and made available to the public, which in turn helps enhance global cybersecurity.

Application Whitelisting

Application whitelisting is a cybersecurity strategy where a list of software applications that are allowed to run on a system or network is explicitly defined and enforced. Only software that has been verified as safe and necessary for business operations is included on the whitelist, while all other software is blocked by default. This is the opposite approach of application blacklisting, which involves creating a list of banned applications that cannot be executed, while allowing all other software to run.

Importance of Application Whitelisting:
1. Enhanced Security Posture: By only allowing pre-approved applications to run, whitelisting significantly reduces the risk of malware infections. Since most malware is not on the whitelist, it simply cannot execute, thereby providing a strong layer of protection against many forms of cyber-attacks.

2. Prevention of Unauthorized Applications: Whitelisting helps in preventing employees from using unauthorized applications that may not be secure or could reduce productivity. This includes unlicensed software, potentially unwanted programs (PUPs), or any tool that isn't deemed necessary for the user's role.

3. Compliance and Governance: Many regulatory frameworks recommend or require application whitelisting as part of compliance standards. This is especially true in industries handling sensitive information, where application whitelisting can help in ensuring that only compliant software is used.

4. Reduced Attack Surface: Application whitelisting minimizes the attack surface by limiting the number of active software that could potentially be exploited by attackers. This makes it harder for attackers to find vulnerabilities to exploit.

5. Simplified Software Management: While setting up a whitelist can initially be labor-intensive; it simplifies ongoing software management. Administrators have a clear inventory of authorized software, making it easier to manage updates, patches, and licensing.

6. Targeted Software Usage and Efficiency: Whitelisting encourages efficient use of software, as only tools that are necessary for business operations are allowed. This can also lead to cost savings by avoiding unnecessary software purchases.

However, it's important to note that application whitelisting is not a silver bullet for cybersecurity. It should be part of a layered security approach, as attackers can potentially exploit vulnerabilities within whitelisted applications. Additionally, maintaining an up-to-date whitelist can be challenging in environments where users require frequent access to new software. Proper implementation involves balancing security needs with operational flexibility to avoid hindering productivity.

Application Blacklisting

Application blacklisting is a more traditional and widespread approach compared to whitelisting. It involves creating a list of applications that are not allowed to run on a system or network. Any application on this blacklist is blocked from executing, while all other applications not on the list are allowed to run. This method is commonly used to prevent known malicious or unauthorized software from running.

Key Points:

- Proactive Defense Against Known Threats: Blacklisting helps protect against known malware and software deemed unsuitable for the business environment.

- Flexibility: Users can run any application not specifically blocked, offering greater flexibility than whitelisting.

- Ease of Management: Initially easier to manage than whitelisting, especially in environments where users require a wide range of software for their tasks.

However, the effectiveness of blacklisting is limited in the face of new, unknown threats (zero-day attacks) because only known threats can be added to the blacklist. As a result, blacklisting is often used in conjunction with other security measures.

Application Greylisting

Application greylisting is a less common approach that sits between whitelisting and blacklisting. In this method, newly encountered applications that have not been explicitly approved (whitelisted) or banned (blacklisted) are temporarily restricted or limited in some way until a decision can be made about their trustworthiness. During the greylisting period, the application might be allowed to run in a sandbox environment, monitored for behavior, or subjected to additional checks to determine if it should be moved to the whitelist or blacklist.

Key Points:

- Dynamic Response to Unknown Applications: Greylisting allows for the evaluation of applications before making a definitive security decision.

- Balances Security and Usability: It provides a middle ground, allowing users to potentially access a broader range of applications without immediately exposing the system to the full risk of unvetted software.

- Enhanced Detection of Zero-Day Threats: By monitoring the behavior of greylisted applications, organizations can better detect and respond to new threats.

Greylisting requires more sophisticated management and monitoring systems to analyze the behavior of greylisted applications effectively. It can be more resource-intensive but offers a dynamic way to handle unknown software, balancing operational needs with security concerns.

Proxy Servers

A proxy server acts as an intermediary between end-users and the internet. When a user requests a webpage or any online resource, the request is routed through the proxy server, which then connects to the requested site on behalf of the user, retrieves the content, and forwards it back to the user. This process has several benefits:

- Privacy and Anonymity: By masking the user's IP address, a proxy provides a level of privacy and can protect users from targeted attacks.

- Enhanced Security: Proxies can be used to filter out malicious web traffic, reducing the risk of malware infections. They can also encrypt web requests, providing additional security for data in transit.

- Content Caching: Proxy servers can cache popular websites, making them faster to access for the entire network. This reduces bandwidth usage and improves loading times for frequently accessed sites.

- Access Control and Policy Enforcement: Proxies can enforce organizational policies by restricting access to certain websites or online services, based on various criteria such as user, time, or content category.

URL Filtering

URL filtering is a technique used to block access to certain websites based on their URL. It is often implemented as part of a broader web filtering strategy, which can also include keyword filtering and file type blocking. URL filtering is important for:

-Preventing Access to Inappropriate Content: Organizations use URL filtering to block access to websites that contain inappropriate, harmful, or non-work-related content, in order to maintain a professional work environment.

-Mitigating Cybersecurity Risks: By blocking websites known to distribute malware or engage in phishing, URL filtering reduces the risk of security breaches.

-Regulatory Compliance: For organizations subject to regulatory requirements, URL filtering helps ensure compliance by preventing access to sites that might contain illegal or regulated content.

- Productivity Enhancement: Limiting access to non-business-related websites can reduce distractions and increase productivity among employees.

DMZ

A DMZ, or Demilitarized Zone, in the context of network security, is a physical or logical subnetwork that contains and exposes an organization's external-facing services to an untrusted network, typically the internet. The purpose of a DMZ is to add an additional layer of security to an organization's local area network (LAN); by isolating the external-facing services from the rest of the network, it helps to prevent unauthorized access to the internal network.

Key Characteristics of a DMZ:
- Isolation: The DMZ is a separate network segment, distinct from the internal network and the internet. This segregation is crucial for mitigating the risk of external attacks reaching the internal network.

- Limited Access: Systems within the DMZ have strictly controlled access. They can communicate with the internet and, in a more limited capacity, with the internal network. Rules are configured to ensure that if a DMZ service is compromised, attackers cannot easily pivot to the internal network.

- Monitoring and Logging: Traffic to and from the DMZ is closely monitored and logged. This helps in detecting suspicious activities and mitigating threats promptly.

- Security Policies: Strong security policies, including regular updates and patches, are enforced for systems within the DMZ to protect against vulnerabilities.

Common Uses of a DMZ:
- Web Servers: Hosting websites accessible from the internet, serving as the public face of the organization while protecting the internal network.

- Email Servers: Processing incoming and outgoing emails while isolating the internal network from email-borne threats.

- FTP Servers: Allowing file transfers to and from the organization, while keeping the internal network segregated.

- Application Gateways: Providing a controlled interface for external users to access certain internal applications, often through a web portal.

Implementation:
- Physical DMZ: Implemented using separate physical hardware and network devices, offering a high level of security by physically segregating network segments.

- Virtual DMZ: Utilizes virtualization technology to create isolated network segments within the same physical network infrastructure. This approach is more flexible and cost-effective but requires careful configuration to ensure security.

Security Considerations:
While a DMZ adds an important security layer, it is not infallible. Each service hosted in the DMZ represents a potential entry point for attackers. Therefore, services within the DMZ need to be securely configured, regularly updated, and monitored for suspicious activities. Additionally, the principle of least privilege should be applied, ensuring that DMZ systems have only the access and resources necessary to perform their intended functions.

In summary, a DMZ is a critical component of a network's security architecture, designed to provide a buffer zone that mitigates the risk of external threats reaching the internal network, while allowing the organization to offer necessary services to users on the internet.

9798320499598